METHUEN'S OLD ENGLISH LIBRARY

General Editors:

A. H. SMITH, Quain Professor of English, University College, London;
and F. NORMAN, Professor of German, King's College, London

THE BATTLE OF MALDON

THE CAUSEWAY OR 'HARD' WITH NORTHEY ISLAND IN THE BACKGROUND

THE BATTLE OF
MALDON

By

E. V. GORDON

FORMERLY SMITH PROFESSOR OF ENGLISH LANGUAGE AND
GERMANIC PHILOLOGY IN THE UNIVERSITY
OF MANCHESTER

New York

APPLETON-CENTURY-CROFTS
Division of Meredith Publishing Company

PREFACE

The Battle of Maldon is now for the first time edited from
the transcript of John Elphinston. Hearne's print of
1726 has hitherto been regarded as the sole authority for
the text, the only Old English manuscript known to
contain a copy having been destroyed in the Cottonian
fire of 1731. Elphinston's transcript was only recently
identified by Mr. N. R. Ker, who has generously allowed
me to profit by his discovery. This transcript enables
the editor to eliminate the misreadings of Hearne's print,
and although the number of these is not large, it is of some
importance even to establish Hearne's accuracy and bring
the text one step nearer the original manuscript. In this
edition an attempt has been made also to provide some
new information about Byrhtnoth and his followers, and
the Scandinavian leaders in the battle, and to give a fresh
valuation of the literary worth of the poem—enough, it
is hoped, to justify a new edition of this text.

It is an innovation that the text is printed in unbroken
long lines, that is, without any extra space after the first
hemistich. This arrangement seems to me to improve
the appearance of the printed page, and it has the important
advantage of bringing out the fluency of the rhythm—
especially notable in this poem. I believe that all Old
English poetry, over-punctuated and needlessly broken
in most of our editions, would gain from being printed
in this form.

References throughout the edition will give some idea
of my indebtedness to previous editors and commentators. In particular, I wish to acknowledge the value of
Miss Ashdown's edition, and of the historical studies in

Napier and Stevenson's *Crawford Charters*. I recognize also the importance of Dr. E. D. Laborde's discovery of the site of the battlefield ; his article, published in 1925, has made intelligible many references in the poem which had puzzled or misled earlier students. But I owe my greatest debt of gratitude to Miss F. E. Harmer and Professor J. R. R. Tolkien, who read the proofs of my edition and made many corrections and contributions. In the assessment of evidence from historical documents especially Miss Harmer's guidance has been invaluable ; and Professor Tolkien, with characteristic generosity, gave me the solution to many of the textual and philological problems discussed in the following pages. I also wish to thank Mr. C. L. Wrenn, who gave me the benefit of his views on several difficult points of interpretation, Dr. Robin Flower, who examined the surviving fragments of the old manuscript and gave his expert opinion on the dating of the hands, and my wife, for her very helpful criticism.

E. V. GORDON

VICTORIA UNIVERSITY, MANCHESTER
March 1937

CONTENTS

ILLUSTRATIONS

ABBREVIATIONS

When an author's name is cited alone further details of his work will be found in the Bibliography.

Archiv	. .	(*Herrigs*) *Archiv für das Studium der Neueren Sprachen und Litteraturen*
ASC .	. .	*Anglo-Saxon Chronicle*
Ashdown .	.	M. Ashdown, *English and Norse Documents*, 1930
BCS .	. .	W. de G. Birch, *Cartularium Saxonicum*, 1885–93
BT .	. .	J. Bosworth and T. N. Toller, *An Anglo-Saxon Dictionary*, 1882–98 (Suppl. 1908–21)
Crawford Ch	.	*The Crawford Charters*, ed. A. S. Napier and W. H. Stevenson, 1895
DNB	. .	*Dictionary of National Biography*
E .	. .	Elphinston's transcript of *The Battle of Maldon*
H .	. .	Hearne's print of *The Battle of Maldon*
KCD	. .	J. M. Kemble, *Codex Diplomaticus Aevi Saxonici*, 1839–48
Luick	. .	K. Luick, *Historische Grammatik der englischen Sprache*, 1921
Maldon	. .	the poem on the battle of Maldon
ME .	. .	Middle English
MLR	. .	*Modern Language Review*
NED	. .	*New English Dictionary*
OE .	. .	Old English
OEScand .	.	Old East Scandinavian
OFris	. .	Old Frisian
OHG	. .	Old High German
ON .	. .	Old Norse
OWScand .	.	Old West Scandinavian
Sedgefield .	.	W. J. Sedgefield, *The Battle of Maldon*, [1904]
Sievers	. .	E. Sievers, *Angelsächsische Grammatik* (3rd ed.) transl. A. S. Cook, *Old English Grammar*
Whitelock .	.	D. Whitelock, *Anglo-Saxon Wills*, 1930

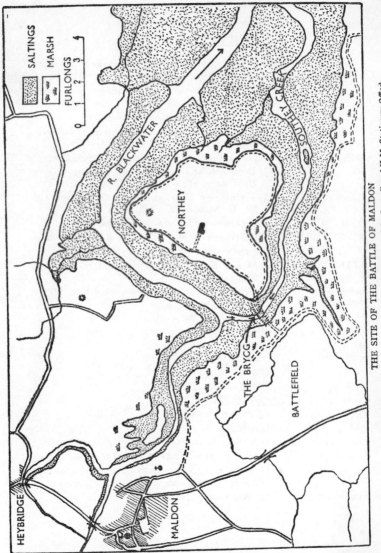

THE SITE OF THE BATTLE OF MALDON

(Based upon Ordnance Survey Map 6" Essex 54, by permission of the Controller of H.M. Stationery Office)

INTRODUCTION

THE BATTLE

THE battle of Maldon was fought in 991,[1] when a viking fleet which had plundered the coast of Kent and sacked Ipswich sailed up the estuary of the Blackwater and established a base near Maldon. The vikings found their passage across the Blackwater opposed by Byrhtnoð, ealdorman of Essex, with his household following and the *fyrd* of the East Saxons. *The Battle of Maldon* relates how the English easily prevented the vikings' attempt to cross, and how Byrhtnoð, magnanimous and over-confident, allowed them passage ; how disaster then befell the English—the death of Byrhtnoð and the flight of Godric and many men of the *fyrd*, and the heroic resistance of Byrhtnoð's own followers to the death. A fierce and hard-fought battle, that cost the men of Essex dear, it was not of great historical importance, having no effect upon the tide of Scandinavian invasion which was about to rise in flood once again around England's shores.

The leaders of these vikings, we are told by Florence of Worcester [2] and Symeon of Durham,[2] were Justin and Guðmund Steitan sunu, and it is possible, though doubtful, that their chief leader was the great Olaf Tryggvason, afterwards (995–1000) king of Norway, and the hero of a famous saga.[3] The Justin of the English docu-

[1] On 10 August, according to Byrhtnoð's *obit* in a twelfth-century Ely calendar, now in the Library of Trinity College, Cambridge. See B. Dickins, *Leeds Studies in English* vi. (1937), p. 14 ff.

[2] Sub anno dccccxci. Their account follows the entry in ASC (versions CDE, see below, p. 10) in the main, but adds the names of these leaders, derived from some unknown source.

[3] The problem is discussed below, p. 10 f. For editions and translations of *Ólafs saga Tryggvasonar*, see p. 65.

ments appears in this saga of Olaf as Jósteinn, and he is Olaf's maternal uncle ; he had sailed from Norway to look for Olaf. Thus, whether Olaf was present at the battle or not, it is likely that the vikings who came to the neighbourhood of Maldon were in the main a Norwegian force. When the Old English poet calls them *Dene* ' Danes ' (line 129), he is following the common habit of his countrymen in applying this name indiscriminately to all Scandinavians.

It is not immediately obvious why the vikings found it necessary to cross the river Blackwater at a place where their passage was so easily preventable. Two suggestions of sites have been offered to explain this necessity, and to clarify the various references to local conditions in the poem. Freeman, *Norman Conquest* I. 271, thought that the vikings were on the south side of the river, on ground north of the town of Maldon and above the estuary, while Byrhtnoð ' came to the rescue from the north ' and ' seems to have halted on the spot now occupied by the church of Heybridge '. The old bridge there is supposed to be on the site of the *bricʒ* mentioned in the poem (ll. 74, 78), which the vikings had to cross before they could reach the English. Freeman's localization of the battle must be rejected, because it clearly does not accord with the details given in the poem, where it is said that the vikings crossed westwards over the river (*þest ofer Pantan* 97). Freeman's notion that one of the vikings threw a spear from the south was derived from misinterpretation of *superne ʒar* in 134 ; the spear was not thrown from the south, but was of southern make (see 134 note). It is evident also that the *bricʒ* of the poem was not the normal type of bridge that existed at Heybridge, but was somehow a ford as well as a bridge, some means of crossing which could not be used at high tide. The vikings had to wait until the tide had ebbed before they could attempt to cross the bridge (ll. 64–78), and when they were allowed to cross, they did not walk dryshod, but waded through the water (l. 96). The term *bricʒ* in 74 and 78 must refer to the same means of crossing as the *ford* of 81 and 88. A further objection to Freeman's theory is that the vikings on the bank south of Heybridge could easily have found fords by going a short way upstream.

These difficulties disappear in the more recent hypothesis of E. D. Laborde.[1] He supposes that the vikings had sailed up the broad tidal estuary of the Blackwater to the island of Northey [2] at its western (upper) extremity, and encamped on it. The island provided them with a base safe from attack, just such a place as other viking forces are known to have chosen [3] ; but it did not give them ready access to the mainland. The only means of reaching the mainland was a ford stretching in a south-westerly direction from the western point of the island across the southern branch of the estuary (now called Southey Creek). The ridge which formed the basis of this ford was probably partly exposed at low tide, and already in Anglo-Saxon times may have been made more serviceable by the addition of stones. In modern times it has been built up into a ' hard ' or causeway which can be crossed by farm vehicles, but it is still covered at high tide just as it was at the time of the battle (see the frontispiece). The causeway is now about 8 feet wide and about 80 yards in length. The channel is thus not too wide for speakers who shouted to be heard across it (as in the poem, ll. 29–61).

This causeway which was also a ford can be acceptably identified with the *bricʒ* of the poem which was also a ford. The use of the term *bricʒ* for such a means of crossing is not unparalleled in Old English.[4] Dr. Laborde's

[1] *English Historical Review* xl. 161 f (1925).

[2] Formerly *Siʒerices eʒ* : P. H. Reaney, *Place-names of Essex* 218.

[3] For example, in 855 the Danes had the isle of Sheppey as their base; in 893 they took refuge on Thorney in the river Colne, and others made a base on the island of Mersea in the same year ; in 918 vikings made the island of Flatholme in the Severn estuary their base.

[4] Passages cited in BT (supplement) under *brycʒ* show that the word could be applied to any formation such as a causeway, or

localization gives full force to the statement of the poem that the vikings crossed *pest ofer Pantan*, and provides a specific meaning for the otherwise uncertain phrase *lucon laʒustreamas* (l. 66), which would be an apt description of the meeting of the two tidal streams flowing up the channels around the island and coming together at its western end in full sight of the two armies drawn up by the ford. The description, at the beginning of the fragment, of the young English gallant passing the time by hawking fits into the scene chosen, as the muddy, shallow banks of the Blackwater attract numerous water-fowl and would be an ideal hawking-ground.[1] The wood to which the hawk flew when released, and to which Godric and others fled, is not two miles away behind the English position.

It is now easy to see why the vikings were forced to cross the river at this point and were not able to move off and find an unprotected passage elsewhere. There is no other ford from the island, and they could not use their ships to cross, because the water is very shallow for some distance out from the bank, even at high tide. The only ways in which the ships could move would be up and down the deep channels in the centre. Byrhtnoð was able to keep the vikings bottled up on the island as long as he held the ford ; the alternative for the vikings would be to embark and sail away, and there was no good landing-place close at hand, except higher up under the fortress of Maldon.[2]

The account of the battle in the poem, in so far as its statements can be checked, is accurate in every particular. The seemingly contradictory details of the passage across

stepping-stones, or planks laid on the ground to provide a good crossing over boggy ground or mud. The verbs *brycʒian, ʒebrycʒian* could similarly mean ' to make a causeway ' and were used of covering a muddy road with any substance that made it more passable. For a similar modern use see NED s.v. *bridge*, sense 4.

[1] Cf the passages in NED s.v. *river*, sense 2.

[2] Maldon had been fortified since 920, as ASC (A) records: *Her . . . for Eadpeard cyninʒ to Mældune 7 ʒetimbrede þa burʒ 7 ʒestaðolode ær he þonon fore.*

4

the river are explained by reference to the site, and the information about the persons who took part in the battle seems to be correct. Byrhtnoð, the English leader, was in truth a *har hilderinc* (l. 169) in 991 : he must then have been about sixty-five (see below, p. 17). All that the poem tells of him, his impetuousness, his hard fighting, his rash magnanimity, his deep religious feeling, accords with what is known from other sources. Several of his followers who are named can be identified, Wulfstan, Wulfmær se ʒeonʒa, and Ælfwine practically with certainty, others less certainly.[1] Many of the details cannot be checked, but the poem gives the impression of being the work of a man well acquainted with the topography of the battlefield, the character and the history of the English leaders, and all the events of the battle. His account as a whole, too, is reasonable and consistent, and free from the exaggerations and high-flown language found in later accounts. How much the poet knew about the vikings is uncertain : he does not mention any of their leaders, but it would be rash to infer that he did not know who they were (see below, p. 22).

The poem is the important record of the battle : it is the only detailed account, and, except for the brief notice in Chronicles CDEF under 991, it is the only one that is generally trustworthy. The most valuable of the other records is that contained in the *Vita Oswaldi*, written between 997 and 1005.[2] The author was probably a monk of Ramsey, and as a contemporary residing in a monastery where Byrhtnoð was personally known and respected, he should have been well informed

---

[1] It is difficult to estimate the probability of the suggested identifications of Byrhtwold, the brothers Sibyrht and Æðeric, and the brothers Oswold and Eadwold (see Glossary of Proper Names), but there is a general likelihood that any Essex landowner of military age, like Sibyrht and Æðeric, would be in Byrhtnoð's following at the battle. The identification of Byrhtwold receives some support from the use of the epithet ʒeneat in l. 310, but the identification of the last two is no more than a guess.

[2] On the dating see F. Liebermann, Archiv ci. 23, note 52.

about Byrhtnoð and his fate. His love of rhetoric and his desire to glorify Byrhtnoð have seduced him to exaggerations, yet his picture of Byrhtnoð in battle is vivid and in the main true enough. We shall have occasion to refer again to his account, which is worth quoting in full :

Transactis non plurimis mensibus,[1] factum est et aliud fortissimum bellum in oriente hujus inclytae regionis,[2] in quo primatum pugnae tenuit gloriosus dux Byrihtnodus cum commilitonibus suis. Quam gloriose, quamque viriliter, quam audacter incitavit principes belli suos ad aciem, quis urbanitate fretus potest edicere ? Stabat ipse, statura procerus, eminens super caeteros, cujus manum non Aaron et Hur sustentabant, sed multimoda pietas Domini fulciebat, quoniam ipse dignus erat. Percutiebat quoque a dextris, non reminiscens cigneam canitiem sui capitis, quoniam elemosinae et sacrae Missae eum confortabant. Protegebat se a sinistris debilitationem oblitus sui corporis, quem orationes et bonae actiones elevabant. Cumque pretiosus campi ductor cerneret inimicos ruere et suos viriliter pugnare, eosque multipliciter caedere, tota virtute coepit pro patria pugnare. Ceciderunt enim ex illis et nostris infinitus numerus, et Byrihtnothus cecidit, et reliqui fugerunt. Dani quoque mirabiliter sunt vulnerati, qui vix suas constituere naves poterant hominibus.[3]

Here is independent corroboration of many details of the poem : Byrhtnoð in the thick of the fight, inciting his followers to the front of battle (4, 127, 170) ; his white hair (169) ; his piety (170 f) ; his carelessness of his own bodily weakness (168) ; and the widespread flight following his death is confirmed (185, 195, 239–43). Two details not in the poem are added, Byrhtnoð's great stature, and the bloody slaughter on both sides. The account of both is probably founded on fact.[4]

[1] After a victory had been won over the Danes in Devonshire ; but this battle was more than a few months earlier. It is recorded in the Chronicle under 988.

[2] In the context *hujus regionis* should refer to Devonshire, but is perhaps used of England as a whole, or of the region in which the author is writing.

[3] *Historians of the Church of York*, ed. J. Raine (1886), I. 455 ; the passage is translated in Sedgefield, p. xi.

[4] Though the statement that ' The Danes . . . scarcely had men enough left to man the ships ' is certainly an exaggeration. The

The account in *Liber Eliensis* of Byrhtnoð's stand is fuller, and in some respects nearer the tradition of the poem than the *Vita Oswaldi* ; but it is much less accurate. This is not surprising, as it belongs to a considerably later date ; the history as a whole is the work of Thomas, a monk of Ely, writing about 1170 ; but he has founded it on the history of Richard, written c. 1130,[1] often transcribing whole sections verbatim from Richard. The real author of the chapter on Byrhtnoð (II. 62) is more likely to be Richard, since the writer says that he is drawing his information about Byrhtnoð's life and deeds from *historiae* in the English tongue ; and Richard s interest in English stories about heroes is known.[2] These *historiae* about Byrhtnoð evidently differed considerably from the Old English poem, but may have been ultimately derived from it. In the Ely historian's summary of these stories, Byrhtnoð has become *Northanimbrorum dux*, and he is said to have fought two battles at Maldon. In the first he was victorious, slaying almost all the vikings on the bridge over the river. The second battle of Maldon, in which he fell, was four years later and lasted fourteen days. On his way to the battlefield, when he ' made all haste to prevent the hostile force from occupying a single foot's length of ground ', his men were refused hospitality by the Abbot of Ramsey, but were welcomed by the Abbot of Ely. Byrhtnoð took the incident as a test of the merit of the two abbeys, and made great presents of land to Ely. In the battle which followed Byrhtnoð attacked the vikings under Justin and Guthmund with an inferior force, but made a great slaughter ; yet by the fourteenth day few of the English were left alive. The

vikings were so far from being crippled as a fighting force that they were able to continue plundering along the coasts and exact a payment of ten thousand pounds from the English, as we learn from ASC (CDEF).

[1] F. Liebermann, Archiv ci. 26.

[2] Richard was the author of *Gesta Herewardi*, using sources in English.

Danes attacked in a wedge formation and succeeded in cutting off Byrhtnoð's head as he fought, and they took the head away with them to their own country. After the battle, the Abbot of Ely went to the field with some of his monks and took up the hero's body, burying it in his church with a round lump of wax where the head should have been.[1]

It looks as if popular imagination, that is, makers of stories using oral tradition, had been at work, confusing and exaggerating the events of the hero's last battle. There are details in the Ely summary that echo features of the narrative in the poem, but none are remembered in the right connexion, and most of them not in quite the right form. Thus Byrhtnoð actually had some connexion with Northumbria, but here he is wrongly made ealdorman of Northumbria ; he repulses the viking attack on a bridge, but it is a different sort of bridge ; the struggle has the same phases as in the old poem, successful defence followed by stern struggle and defeat, but the first phase is made into a separate battle ; there is a challenging message from the vikings to battle on the field near Maldon, but no request to be allowed to cross the river ; Byrhtnoð resolves that the vikings shall not occupy a single foot of ground, the same phrase that Leofsunu uses in the poem, when he vows that he will not *fleon fotes trym* (247) ; at the end of the battle there is a desperate stand by a few survivors, but Byrhtnoð should not be included among them ; the vikings fight in wedge-formation, which reminds us of the *bordpeall* of the poem (277). The story of Byrhtnoð's requests for hospitality to the two Abbots alone seems to have no basis in old tradition, except that it is not entirely out of harmony with the actual character of Byrhtnoð ; it is a comparatively late fiction.[2] All

---

[1] For the full text see D. J. Stewart's edition of *Liber Eliensis*, pp. 180–3 ; it is translated in Sedgefield, pp. xviii f.

[2] Among several indications it is pointed out by F. Liebermann (Archiv ci.) that the Abbot of Ramsey named in this anecdote, Wulsige, did not become abbot until after Byrhtnoð's death.

these alterations and additions are in the vein of popular
romance, and it seems very probable that an English
heroic romance, founded on Old English tradition of
Byrhtnoð and his last battle, perhaps on the known poem,
was the chief source of this chapter of *Liber Eliensis*. And
one fact at least the Ely tradition has preserved correctly :
the burial of the headless body of Byrhtnoð at Ely. There
is early evidence that Byrhtnoð was buried there : his
widow Ælflæd in her will mentions *Æliȝ . . . þer mines
hlafordes lichoma rest* (BCS 1289, Whitelock xv. 40/5).
That the body was actually headless also does not lack
confirmation (see below, p. 21). Other details in the
Ely history, such as Byrhtnoð's championship of the
monks, the names of the viking leaders and the date of
the battle, all given with precise accuracy, are probably
from older documents.

The still later notice of Byrhtnoð and the battle in the
history of Ramsey (written about 1175) is of no further
value. It tells, with a few variations, the story of the Abbot
of Ramsey's refusal to entertain Byrhtnoð and his men ;
the Ramsey historian indicates that the monks of Ely were
quick to see the material advantage of winning the great
man's favour ; ' nevertheless, afterwards being wounded
in battle and near unto death, he made a will leaving us a
hide of land at *Dodinton*, not wishing to seem quite
unmindful of his early affection '.

Some record of the battle must also have been made
on the tapestry which Ælflæd wove after Byrhtnoð's death,
with his deeds depicted on it. This *cortinam gestis viri
sui intextam atque depictam in memoriam probitatis ejus* [1]
she gave to the church at Ely. It has not survived to the
present day, but may have been still in existence, together
with other treasures received from Byrhtnoð and his wife,
when the Ely monks wrote their history.

[1] *Liber Eliensis* II. 63, ed. D. J. Stewart, p. 183.

9

THE BATTLE OF MALDON

OLAF TRYGGVASON AND THE BATTLE OF MALDON

It seems to be the common faith of students of *Maldon*
that the leader of the vikings was Olaf Tryggvason ; and
because it is surprising that the poet did not mention a
commander so famous, some have concluded that he composed the poem so soon after the battle that he did not yet
know that Anlaf (Olaf) was the leader of the enemy.[1]
The idea that Olaf was the viking commander was derived
primarily from the statement of version A of the *Anglo-
Saxon Chronicle.*

993. Her on ðissum ʒeare com Unlaf [2] mid þrim 7 hundniʒ-
entiʒon scipum to Stane,[3] 7 forherʒedon þæt on ytan, 7 for þa
ðanon to Sandpíc,[4] 7 spa ðanon to ʒipespíc,[5] 7 þæt eall ofereode,
7 spa to Mældune [6] ; 7 him þær com toʒeanes Byrhtnoð ealdorman
mid his fyrde, 7 him pið ʒefeaht. 7 hy þone ealdorman þær ofsloʒon,
7 pælstope ʒepeald ahtan. 7 him man nam syððan frið pið, 7
hine nam se cinʒ syððan to bisceopes handa [ðurh Sirices lare
Cantpare biscpes 7 Ælfeaʒes Pincæstre biscpes].[7]

Yet this version has misdated the event by two years,
and, perhaps as a result, it has mingled events belonging
to 991 with events belonging to 994. Olaf's confirmation
quite certainly belongs to 994, where it is correctly recorded
in the other versions of the chronicle, and it may be that
other matter also has been taken over from 994. The
other versions of the Chronicle say nothing about Olaf
at Maldon :

991. Her [pæs ʒypespic ʒeherʒod, 7 æfter þam spiðe raðe] pæs
Brihtnoð [Byrihtnoð D] ofslæʒen æt Mældune, 7 on þam ʒeare man
ʒerædde þæt man ʒeald ærest ʒafol Deniscum mannum, for þam
miclan broʒan þe hi porhton be þam særiman. þæt pæs ærest .x.
þusend punda. þæne ræd ʒerædde Siric arcebiscop.[8]

The same versions begin the annal 994 thus : Her . . .
com Anlaf 7 Speʒen to Lunden byriʒ . . . mid .iiii. 7

[1] H. Sweet, *Anglo-Saxon Reader*, p. 120, citing Rieger.
[2] OE *Unlaf, Anlaf* = later Norse *Ólafr.* [3] Folkestone. [4] Sand-
wich. [5] Ipswich. [6] Maldon. [7] A late addition.
[8] Except for minor variations of spelling, this represents the annal
in C, D and E. F omits the passage in brackets.

10

hundniȝontiȝon scipum. Thus it looks as if A's record
of Unlaf's coming with 93 ships is simply an inaccurate
echo of Anlaf's coming in 994 with 94 ships [1] (iiii having
been misread as iii), especially as we know that at least one
other event of 994 was transferred to that annal. It is
in fact generally agreed by editors and commentators [2]
that 993 A is an amalgam of events belonging to 991 and
994; yet this conclusion has by no means settled the
Olaf question.

Another document commonly adduced as proof of Olaf's
presence at Maldon is a text of a treaty between King
Æðelred and a viking fleet commanded by Anlaf, Justin
and Guðmund Stegitan sunu.[3] This treaty is not dated
in the document, but it must belong either to 991 or
994; and it has usually been assigned to 991,[4] mainly
for negative reasons. The problem is too complex to
be discussed at length here, but an attempt has been
made elsewhere (MLR xxxii. 24) to show that the pro-
visions of the treaty apply more aptly to the conditions
of 994 than to 991. The terms do not apply naturally
to 991: they are quite general, intended to cover relations
between the vikings of the fleet and the English throughout
the country, without specific application to Kent or Essex;
and it seems likely, from the Chronicle evidence, that the
truce of 991 was a local agreement arranged by Sigeric
(not the king) on behalf of these districts. If the truce
made in 991 was general, Olaf was undoubtedly the leader
of the viking fleet, on the evidence of the treaty document,
and we must then admit that he violated the treaty by
plundering various parts of England during the following

---

[1] A fleet of this size implies a fighting force of 2000 to 2500 men.
If this was the united force of Swegen and Olaf, the viking army at
Maldon must have been considerably smaller.

[2] By F. Liebermann, C. Plummer, and M. Ashdown.

[3] See below, p. 65 (under 1898), and cf above, p. 1.

[4] By Schmid, Freeman, Steenstrup, Napier and Stevenson,
Plummer, Liebermann, and others; Kemble and Worsaae have
favoured 994.

years. Such a blatant breach of faith was not in Olaf's character as we know it from the sagas.

The first clause of the treaty, where the viking leaders are named, also states that Archbishop Sigeric and the ealdormen Æðelweard and Ælfric negotiated with the vikings. As Sigeric died in 994 before the king concluded the treaty in that year, this statement has been adduced as the chief reason for assigning the treaty to 991. But this first clause can be taken more naturally to mean (and this is the crucial point of the argument) that Archbishop Sigeric and the ealdormen Æðelweard and Ælfric had made local truces with the vikings earlier in that year, and that these were confirmed in the general treaty of peace ; now it was only in 994 that Sigeric, Æðelweard and Ælfric would all have occasion to make local truces with the vikings ; it was in that year, according to the Chronicle, that their provinces, Kent, Hampshire, and other parts of Wessex, were ravaged by Olaf. We may note also that the agreed arrangement for provisioning the vikings is similarly stressed in the Chronicle under 994. Nothing is said in the treaty of Swegen, Olaf's partner in his earlier raids of 994, for the reason that Swegen had left Olaf and sailed away to take part in campaigns in Slesvig and Saxony in 994–6.[1] In the Chronicle, too, the negotiations of 994 are solely with Olaf. The terms of the treaty seem to agree more closely with the Chronicle's record of 994 than with its account of the peace made in 991.

A further point against the assumption that Olaf was present at the battle is that, except for the discredited annal 993 in Chronicle A, the only early authorities that name the viking leaders at Maldon—Florence of Worcester, Symeon of Durham, and *Liber Eliensis*—state that they were Justin and Guthmund, and none mentions Olaf. The value of this evidence is, however, difficult to estimate. The three authorities are really one, as Symeon and the Ely monk probably took these names from Florence. If, as seems likely, Florence used the treaty text as one of

[1] J. C. H. R. Steenstrup, *Normannerne* III. 244 f, and below, p. 53.

his sources, it is curious that he omitted Olaf's name. If the omission was deliberate, Florence's testimony is important ; but it may have been merely accidental.[1]

Then there is the evidence of *Ólafs saga Tryggvasonar*. The saga is a considerably later document than those just considered, and its material presents the usual advantages and disadvantages of the sagas as historical evidence. There are several different versions written in the thirteenth and fourteenth centuries, but all are based on the lost Latin history of Oddr Snorrason, compiled about 1190, mainly from oral tradition, or upon Oddr with additions from the slightly later *Ólafs saga* (also lost) by Gunnlaugr Leifsson. The various versions give practically the same account of Olaf in England, and we may assume that all the main facts and most of the details are from traditions first recorded at the end of the twelfth century. Similar accounts are also given more briefly in the twelfth-century *Historia de Antiquitate Regum Norwagiensium* by the Norwegian monk Theodric, and in the thirteenth-century anonymous *Historia Norwegiae*, also written in Norway.[2] The Scandinavian narrative of Olaf's activities in England is comparatively full, but vague about localities and dates, and clearly untrustworthy in many details. Yet when the saga relates that Olaf had been some years in the British Isles before he was baptized, this account has at least some probability, in spite of the *Anglo-Saxon Chronicle*, which introduces him for the first time in 994. The saga tells how Olaf came to take up the viking ventures that brought him to the British Isles, and the full narrative gives some indications of the saga-writer's notion of the dating.[3] After the death

[1] Florence seems to have read Asser and Osbern's account of Bishop Ælfeah in the same manuscript as *Maldon* : see below, p. 33. There is no evidence, however, that he made any use of the poem.

[2] Both ed. G. Storm in *Monumenta Historica Norvegiae*, Kristiania 1880.

[3] These indications have been translated into definite figures by Finnur Jónsson in his edition of Snorri's *Heimskringla* (1893–1901) I. 306 f.

of his wife Geira in 990 he went to Garðaríki, and the next year to Denmark, and thence west on raids to Saxony, Frisia and England. In England he plundered first in the south (no localities specified) and then passed northwards along the coast of Northumberland. We may note, without prejudice, that the Chronicle indicates that the vikings who survived Maldon went afterwards to Northumbria. From Northumbria Olaf went on to Scotland, sailed around the northern promontories and made raids in the Hebrides, Man, Ireland, Wales and Brittany. Most of this itinerary is vouched for by Hallfreðr Vandræða-skáld, Olaf's court poet, in his *Ólafsdrápa*, composed in 996.[1] Hallfreðr refers to Olaf's campaigns only in general terms, and gives no details of the battles. Towards the end of this viking tour Olaf came to the Scilly Isles and was baptized there ; the longer version of the saga gives a definite date for this event, 993, and though there are other accounts of Olaf's baptism, the saga may well be correct. The saga says nothing of his confirmation, however, at Andover in the following year.

In the autumn of 993 Olaf visited a port in the north of England and there married Gyða, sister of Olaf Kvaran, who is said to be king of Dublin at the time.[2] After his marriage Olaf spent his time partly in northern England and partly in Ireland, until messengers from Norway, Þórir klakka and Olaf's uncles Jósteinn (Justin in English documents) and Karlshǫfuð, found him in Dublin in 995 and persuaded him to return to Norway. Nothing is said of Olaf's partnership with Swegen or his campaign in England in 994.

Thus the evidence of the saga, for what it is worth, goes to show that it is unlikely that Olaf and Jósteinn were together in one fleet in 991 ; it would be much more plausible to represent them as being together in 994. The viking force which fought at Maldon would be under the command

---

[1] *Norsk-islandske Skjaldedigtning*, ed. F. Jónsson, III. 150 ; G. Vigfusson and F. Y. Powell, *Corpus Poeticum Boreale* II. 94-5.
[2] Actually Ólafr Kvaran had died in 981.

of Olaf alone, or else under Jósteinn and a fellow-chieftain, who, after plundering in England during 991–3, joined themselves in 994 to Olaf's fleet.

The evidence is of such uncertain nature that we cannot reach any final decision about Olaf's presence or absence at Maldon, but on the whole it seems probable that he was not present at Maldon, and that the treaty containing his name belongs to 994.

BYRHTNOÐ

Byrhtnoð did not spring into fame as the hero of Maldon ; he was one of the great men of his generation, one of the most powerful among the ealdormen, prominent in politics at the time of anti-monastic reaction, and famed as a zealous defender of the monks and of his country. He had a striking personal presence ; he was immensely tall and strong, quick and vigorous of mind, ready of speech and outspoken. Upon occasion he seems to have successfully intimidated the opposition in council ; and in general his later fame shows that he made a deep impression on his own age. Not much is known of his parents, except the name of his father Byrhtelm, but it would appear from his connexions, both of kinship and of marriage, that he was of distinguished family and social importance. Ælfwine, who refers to Byrhtnoð as his mæg [1] in line 224, is the grandson [2] of Ealhelm, who was the ealdorman of Mercia in 940–51. Byrhtnoð's wife Ælflæd was the daughter of Ælfgar, ealdorman of Essex,[3] 946–51. And her sister, Æðelflæd [4]

[1] This usually implies blood relationship.

[2] He refers to Ealhelm as *min ealda fæder* in l. 218 ; for the usage of this phrase see note.

[3] Not of East Anglia, as Liebermann and others have supposed. There was only one *ealdordom* in East Anglia, and it was occupied by Æðelstan up to the time of Ælfgar's death.

[4] This is the Æðelflæd mentioned in *Liber Eliensis*, ii. c. 64, who by a misunderstanding of the passage has usually been regarded as Byrhtnoð's sister. See D. Whitelock, *MLR* 33 (1938), p. 274.

æt Domerhame, married King Eadmund about two years before his death in 946, and survived him. Later she married Æðelstan who was possibly the Æðelstan who was called ' half-king ', ealdorman of East Anglia 923–58, or, perhaps more probably, the younger contemporary who signs as ealdorman from 940 to 974 (see D. Whitelock, *MLR* 33, p. 274). This Æðelflæd æt Domerhame was a lady of great possessions, as is shown by her will (Whitelock xiv), in which she left considerable property to her sister and brother-in-law.

Napier and Stevenson (Crawford Ch, p. 85) have suggested as an ancestor (probably grandfather) of Byrhtnoð that Byrhtsige, son of the *æðelinʒ* Beornoð (Chronicle A) or Beorhtnoð (B, C, D), who fell in 905 fighting rebelliously on the side of the *æðelinʒ* Æðelwold and his East Anglian Danish followers against King Eadweard. If Beornoð is the right name of the father, he was probably an *æðelinʒ* of the Mercian royal house (Crawford Ch, p. 85, n. 4), whose last king Burgred had been driven out by the Danes in 874. Byrhtsige may have felt, like Æðelwold, that he had a claim to royal rank, and had been wrongfully passed over. In any case Byrhtnoð's family was probably of Mercian origin; their lands lay mainly around Cambridge.

Byrhtnoð was made ealdorman of Essex in 956, probably succeeding Byrhtferð, of whom almost nothing is known.[1] His father-in-law Ælfgar, who had also been ealdorman of Essex, had died about 951, and in his will, which was probably made a few years earlier,[2] he refers to Byrhtnoð

---

[1] Chadwick, *Studies in Anglo-Saxon Institutions*, pp. 180, 187, considers it likely that Byrhtferð *dux* was Byrhtnoð's predecessor in Essex, and suggests (p. 293) that he may have been a kinsman of Byrhtnoð. The name of Ælfgar *dux* in charters of 956 and 958 does not belong to Byrhtnoð's father-in-law, and therefore causes no difficulty here (Crawford Ch, p. 86, note 2).

[2] Ælfgar received the king's permission to make his will between 946 and 949 (Whitelock, p. 104), and it is unlikely that he would wait long after receiving this permission.

as then married to Ælflæd. Hence Byrhtnoð was probably married by 947. If we assume that he was then about twenty-one years old, his birth would be in 926. He would be thirty when made an ealdorman, and sixty-five when he fell at Maldon. The poem calls him a *har hilderinc* (169) in the battle, and *Vita Oswaldi* says he is forgetful of the *cigneam canitiem sui capitis*, and that his body is weakened by age (above, p. 6).

Florence of Worcester seems to be the first to define Byrhtnoð's earldom as Essex, but the poem implies it clearly, and there is other evidence. Only the *Liber Eliensis* (and a few later writings depending on the *Liber Eliensis*) describes him as *Northanimbrorum dux*. This title, though inaccurate, is not altogether a baseless fiction, since Byrhtnoð probably had authority of some sort in Northumbria : that is implied by the presence in his following of the noble Northumbrian hostage Æscferð, son of Ecglaf (ll. 265–7). The hostage's family cannot now be identified, and it is impossible to do more than guess at Byrhtnoð's part in Northumbrian affairs.

Byrhtnoð's patrimony of lands in Cambridgeshire and neighbouring counties was extensive, but through his marriage connexions he acquired so much more that he must have been one of the greatest landowners in the country. Much of Ælfgar's considerable estates in Suffolk and Essex came to him, some at Ælfgar's death, and still more at the death of his sister-in-law, Ælfgar's elder daughter Æðelflæd. Our records of Byrhtnoð's lands are incomplete, but we know that he had possessions in Essex, Buckinghamshire, Oxfordshire, Suffolk, Cambridgeshire, Huntingdonshire, Northamptonshire and Worcestershire. No fewer than 39 manors are named in his widow Ælflæd's will, and she had inherited only part of her husband's property. In power Byrhtnoð should probably be ranked next to the two great ealdormen of his time, Ælfhere of Mercia and Æðelwine of East Anglia. His earldom was probably larger than the earlier *ealdordom* of Essex or the modern county, stretching westward far enough to include Oxfordshire.[1] Yet his political strength lay less in wealth and width of territory than in the favour of the king [2] and the church, his firm alliance with powerful friends (especially with Æðelwine of East Anglia), and his popularity as a protector and leader. There could be no more striking testimony of the devotion of his followers than the *Battle of Maldon*. His influence extended into Northumbria and Mercia. *Liber Eliensis* (II. 25) relates that when an unsatisfactory decision about a land claim had been given by the *sapientes et senes* of Huntingdon, ' the whole county was summoned together by ealdorman Byrhtnoð, Ælfwold and Eadric '. Such an action was perhaps not within Byrhtnoð's legal power,[3] and it may be that the account is inaccurate ; but it would be character-istic of Byrhtnoð and his friend Ælfwold not to trouble about legal rights if they thought an injustice had been done.

Byrhtnoð was a deeply religious man, and a generous patron and zealous protector of the monasteries. He worked together with his sister's son Æðelwine in further-ing the reform of the monasteries ; and when Æðelwine and Oswold refounded the abbey of Ramsey, he contributed two of his farms in Northampton towards its support. Ramsey became Æðelwine's favourite monastery, while Ely, in the neighbourhood of Byrhtnoð's family estates, received many benefactions from Byrhtnoð. *Liber Eliensis*

---

[1] At least Oxfordshire and Buckinghamshire were in the jurisdic-tion of his successor Leofsige (KCD 1289) ; see Chadwick, *A.S. Institutions*, p. 177, and *Victoria County History of Essex*, II. 208.

[2] King Eadwig made him ealdorman, Eadgar in a charter made a grant to him as *comiti mihi prae quibusdam ceteris dilecto* (BCS 1134), and as his party was favoured by Æðelred, Byrhtnoð presumably was also personally in favour.

[3] So Liebermann ; but Chadwick, *op. cit.*, pp. 117, note 1, and 413, considers it likely that Byrhtnoð had jurisdiction in Huntingdon-shire. Miss Whitelock (p. 106) takes Chadwick's words to mean that Byrhtnoð was ealdorman there before succeeding to Essex. But he would be a very youthful ealdorman then, unless he was even older than sixty-five in 991.

names fifteen properties given or bequeathed by Byrhtnoð to Ely, while to Ramsey he added to his earlier gift only the manor of Doddington. Comparison of these gifts was the basis of the anecdote related above, pp. 7–9. His widow Ælflæd's will indicates that Byrhtnoð made a grant of land to the community at Mersea, Essex ; and he was probably a benefactor of Abingdon Monastery, Worcester Priory, Christ Church, Canterbury, and the New Minster, Winchester, which recorded the day of his death on its calendar.[1]

After King Eadgar died in 975 a reaction against the reform of the monasteries set in, led by Ælfhere, the ealdorman of Mercia, possibly son of the Ealhelm, and uncle of the Ælfwine mentioned in *The Battle of Maldon*. As the Chroniclers lament in verse, Ælfhere expelled the monks from monasteries in his ealdordom and brought back the canons who were so unmonastic in their way of life that many of them were married. The expulsion of the monks was sometimes carried out at the point of the sword and followed by confiscation of monastic lands. The monks had vigorous defenders in Æðelwine Dei Amicus, his brother Ælfwold, and Byrhtnoð. At a meeting of the *witan* they protested against the expulsion of the monks, and after Æðelwine had presented a reasoned defence of the reform, the more impetuous Byrhtnoð declared that it was not to be endured that the only true upholders of religion in the country should be driven out. After the meeting, according to Florence of Worcester, he and Æðelwine gathered their men and prepared to protect the monasteries under their patronage by force of arms. In a series of meetings in 977 and 978 a compromise was arranged, but it was a compromise more favourable to the monastic party, and the policy of expulsion was checked.

The Ely historian says that Byrhtnoð was ' untiring in his campaigns against the foes of the kingdom ', the vikings, but we are not given any information about his earlier

[1] See Whitelock, pp. 106–7, and F. Liebermann, *Archiv* ci. 16.

campaigns. We are only told that when the Danes carried their devastations into the various districts of the country, ' the men of these districts placed themselves under the guidance of Byrhtnoð as of an invincible patron, so that under his protection they might defend themselves the better against the enemy'. The account in the poem shows him as an experienced leader. He saw the strategic importance of the ford and brought his army up in time to bar it against the vikings. He was familiar with the details of the shield-wall formation, and knew how to place his forces.

It is a remarkable testimony to Byrhtnoð's fame and popularity, to the impression he had made on the people by his deeds and bearing, that he was still celebrated as a hero in the east of England in the twelfth century (above, p. 7). Few of the heroes of times older than the eleventh century were remembered in England after the Conquest, as far as extant literature gives us evidence. Byrhtnoð shares the distinction with the kings Alfred and Æðelstan and the Scandinavian heroes Ólafr Kvaran and Skarði. By the monks of Ely he was also venerated as one of their greatest benefactors and as an heroic defender of the church. Although this veneration might be expected to magnify the hero's virtues in the eyes of the Ely historian, his praise is on the whole merited and his characterization just : ' He was eloquent, robust, of great bodily stature . . . and remarkably brave and free from the fear of death. On all occasions he respected Holy Church and the servants of God, and devoted the whole of his patrimony to their use. He devoted his life while it lasted to the defence of his country's freedom.'

Byrhtnoð's body was taken from the battle-field by the Abbot and monks of Ely and buried in their church. According to tradition the head had been cut off and taken away by the vikings, and the Ely history says that the body was buried with a round lump of wax where the head should have been. The final redactor of the history, Thomas, adds that the body ' was recognized long after-

wards by this sign '. This was probably when the benefactors of the abbey were removed from the Saxon church
and re-interred in the Norman Cathedral of Ely in 1154,
in the historian Thomas's own time. The coffins containing
the remains were afterwards placed in the north wall of
the choir, where they were discovered in the eighteenth
century. They were moved to Bishop West's chapel, and
at the time of the removal Byrhtnoð's bones, taken from
beneath his effigy, were satisfactorily identified. The
following report on his bones, taken from a letter read
before the Society of Antiquaries in 1772, is of great interest for its confirmation of the accounts in *Vita Oswaldi*
and *Liber Eliensis* of Byrhtnoð's missing head and great
stature, though it is difficult to believe that he was as
gigantic as this report would make him :

'I apprised those who attended on that occasion, May 18,
1769, that if my surmises were well founded no head would
be found in the cell which contained the Bones of Brithnoth,
Duke of Northumberland . . . [Under the effigy of]
Duke Brithnoth there were no remains of the head, though
we searched diligently, and found most, if not all his other
bones almost entire, and those remarkable for their length,
and proportionally strong ; which also agrees with what is
recorded by the same historian with regard to the Duke's
person, viz. that he was *viribus robustus, corpore maximus*
. . . It was estimated . . . that the Duke must have
been 6 foot 9 inches in stature. It was observed that the
collar-bone had been nearly cut through, as by a battle-
axe or two-handed sword.' [1]

COMPOSITION AND ART OF THE POEM

The Battle of Maldon was composed soon after the battle :
memory of all that happened was still fresh, and the
heroism of individual deeds and speeches still seemed of
primary importance, their glory undimmed by the defeat.
Soon, even within ten years or so, if the *Vita Oswaldi* is

[1] C. W. Stubbs, *Historical Memorials of Ely Cathedral*, 1897
pp. 92-3, quoted here from M. Ashdown.

fair evidence, the battle was remembered only as a defeat
and as the end of Byrhtnoð ; the other heroes are for-
gotten. The poem impresses all readers as coming not long
after the event. Yet when it is said that it was made so
soon after the battle that the poet did not know the names
even of the viking leaders,[1] we feel that assumption has
been carried too far. Not only is the poem incomplete,
but it is not clear that it was to the poet's purpose to name
the viking leaders. He was occupied with the fate of
the English heroes who were his friends ; their manner of
dying was what mattered, and the vikings were merely
the agent of destruction. Their names might interest a
writer taking a general historical view, but were inessential
to the poet of the heroic defeat.

The poet was probably not present at the battle.
Jehyrde ic ' I heard ' he says of Eadweard's killing a
viking (117), and although the phrase is conventional,
a common epic formula, used to imply that the fame of
the deed was current, it is a formula which the poet would
hardly use if he had seen the deed himself. The subjunctive of the verb following (*sloȝe*), instead of the usual
indicative, seems a deliberate indication that the poet
knew of the deed only from report. Yet though the poet
was not in the battle, it is not unlikely that he knew the
heroes of his poem personally. It can be seen in the great
restraint of his account that he was deeply moved by their
loyal and unflinching end, and he records with care how
the noble retainers kept their vows to their lord. He
tells the whole story from the retainers' point of view, as
is especially noticeable when the poem is compared with
the later accounts of the battle, or with almost any Old
English battle poetry. We can see too that the poet was
well versed in the old heroic and aristocratic traditions of
poetry, and an aristocratic poet in Essex would be certain to
know Byrhtnoð and some of his followers. Possibly he was a
member of Byrhtnoð's well-born *heorðperod*, who missed
the battle and happened to be a practised poet. He

[1] H. Sweet, *Anglo-Saxon Reader*, p. 120, citing Rieger.

composed his poem as a memorial to Byrhtnoð and his noble companions in the same spirit as Byrhtnoð's widow Ælflæd wove her husband's deeds into the tapestry which she gave to Ely.

The aristocratic quality of *Maldon* is evident both in the glorification of the military ideals of the *comitatus* and in the close kinship in art and sentiment with other Old English court poetry. *Maldon* is of the same school as *Beowulf* and nearer to *Beowulf* in heroic art and social feeling than any other Old English poem. The loyal retainers exhort one another to stand by their lord in almost the same words that Wiglaf used to his fellows. They must remember their vows over the mead, and not suffer the disgrace of leaving the battle-field without their lord, says Ælfwine (212 f), and it is an additional motive that Byrhtnoð is his kinsman as well as his lord ; and so Wiglaf had spoken long before, urging his companions to remember their vows at the mead-drinking and go to help Beowulf in his need (*Beowulf* 2633 f ; and kinship appears as a motive in Wiglaf's speech too, in 2600–1). 'This will I vow,' said Leofsunu of Sturmer, 'that I will not flee a single foot hence, but will press on . . .' (246 f)—though knowing the fight hopeless. In almost the same words (in form so close that the *Maldon* text has been used to supply a missing word in *Beowulf*) Beowulf vowed not to turn back from the dragon, but to press on until all was ended by fate (2525). It is significant too that *Beowulf* and *Maldon* are the only Old English poems in which the heroic attitude is fully realized and described.

Then there are the minor epic formulæ, which *Maldon* shares with various poems, but more with *Beowulf* than with any other. Thus for example :

Maldon	*Beowulf*
42 bord hafenode . . . yrre 7 anræd	1573 þæpen hafenade . . . yrre 7 anræd
117 ȝehyrde ic	62 hyrde ic
118 spenȝes ne þyrnde	1520, 2489 hond spenȝ ne ofteah

3

Maldon	Beowulf
225 fæhðe ʒemunde	2488–9 hond ʒemunde fæhðo ʒenoʒe
259 ne for feore murnan	1442 nalles for ealdre mearn
284 seo byrne sanʒ ʒryreleoða sum	1521 on hafelan hrinʒmæl aʒol ʒrædiʒ ʒuðleoð
83 þa hpile þe hi pæpna pealdan moston	2038 þenden hie ðam pæpnum pealdan moston
163 brad 7 brunecʒ	1546 brad [7] brunecʒ
126, 303 pæl feol on eorþan	1042 ðonne palu feollon.

There is no reason to suppose that the *Maldon* poet imitated *Beowulf*, or even that he knew it ; he knew poetry of that kind. His work has parallels also in the *Finnesburh* fragment, and in the martial passages of *Exodus*, *Andreas*, and *Judith*.

Maldon is even more directly in the heroic tradition than *Beowulf* ; it is indeed the only purely heroic poem extant in Old English, since *Finnesburh* and *Waldere* are too fragmentary for their general scope and quality to be gauged. *Beowulf*, usually accounted primarily heroic and epic, is in its ultimate aim elegiac.[1] Being in the direct line of heroic descent, *Maldon* shows a close kinship with poetry of similar ancestry among other Germanic peoples, especially with the heroic poetry of the Scandinavians, much of which is actually contemporary with *Maldon*.

[1] This view raises too large a question to be argued here at length. It may be explained, however, since the structure of *Beowulf* is again referred to on p. 29, that *Beowulf* is regarded as an elegy on the common Old English theme *lif is læne*. The relation of the two parts of the poem is deliberate contrast : the first part shows the hero in his youth at the height of his physical prowess, and contains a series of heroic pictures designed to exhibit his strength and nobility ; the second part shows the sadness of his old age and death, and implies that with him passes the prosperity of his people. Thus all that is noblest in life passes and cannot be replaced. This second part is not merely an additional adventure ; it gives the meaning of the whole poem. There can be no doubt of the essential unity of *Beowulf* : the whole poem is carefully planned to show the tragedy and importance of its elegiac theme. A very similar structure is used also to present an ecclesiastical hero in the poem on Saint Guðlac.

Dame Bertha Phillpotts has called attention (MLR xxiv. 179 f) to a number of striking parallels between *Maldon* and *Bjarkamál* and other Norse poems, in the form of similar phrases, epithets, and expressions of ideas proper to the heroic outlook. She accounts for these similarities by assuming that the *Maldon* poet knew Danish poems and was influenced by them. But since *Maldon* is a thoroughly English poem, closely related in style and feeling to other Old English poems, we are reluctant to admit this even as a possibility, especially as there is no other evidence of Scandinavian influence on the style and form of Old English poetry, though there are many other parallels in phrasing. More probably the parallels found by Dame Bertha Phillpotts are to be explained as survivals from the common poetic tradition of the earlier Germanic heroic age. It is well known that the heroic traditions in both Old English and Old Norse poetry, including heroic ' motives ', conventional phrases, and countless verbal details, were inherited in the main from the migration age. Everything common to *Maldon* and the Norse poems can be explained as part of the common inheritance, made to appear still more striking in *Bjarkamál* by a partial similarity of situation. There was a close connexion between Anglian and Scandinavian culture in the migration age,[1] which might be expected to show itself in closely related traditions for centuries afterwards. Since *Maldon* is the only purely heroic poem in Old English, it is natural that the heroic ideals and details that were the common stock of Germanic tradition should be concentrated more intensely there than in most Old English poetry[2] ; and these traditional matters are present just as naturally in Scandinavian poetry that is primarily heroic.

[1] H. Shetelig, *Préhistoire de la Norvège*, pp. 177, 237–8.
[2] Actually *Beowulf* has a still richer legacy from the heroic age, and is much nearer to Scandinavian poetic tradition than *Maldon*. Dame Bertha Phillpotts' view (MLR xxiv. 186) that *Maldon* has even more in common with *Bjarkamál* than with *Beowulf* is not acceptable.

Much of the heroic tradition of *Maldon*, moreover, goes back to times even earlier than the contact of Angles and Scandinavians in the migration age. It is remarkable that Tacitus' *Germania*, written nearly nine hundred years before Maldon, can often be used as a commentary to explain the sentiments and institutions that lie at the very basis of the heroism of Maldon. Tacitus describes the same military nucleus of society, the chief with his *comitatus*, bound to each other by the closest ties of loyalty; the custom which made it a point of honour for the leaders to fight, like Byrhtnoð, in a conspicuous place in front of the line (cap. vii); the great disgrace incurred by leaving the chief dead on the field and returning lordless home (cap. xiv); the importance of kinship in the military organization (cf the *pinemaȝas* of 306); the special bond between uncle and sister's son (cf note to 115); the patronage of young warriors by the chief (cf 152); and even the same method of fighting in a shield-wall. Strangely enough, the *Battle of Maldon*, composed long after the main interest in Germanic themes had passed away in England, is the clearest and fullest expression known in literature of the ancient Germanic heroic code. The poem should therefore be looked at in this Germanic background; the parallels pointed out by Dame Bertha Phillpotts well illustrate its significance.

The Battle of Maldon does not suffer by comparison with other monuments of Germanic heroic literature, even with the noblest of the Norse sagas and Edda poems. There is none of them that shows a truer understanding of the spirit and code that demanded resistance even when all hope of success was gone and retreat would be wiser. In this poem the reasons for such behaviour were not merely accepted instinctively; they were also intellectually comprehended. In the heroes themselves the source of heroism was the instinctive sense of honour: to live without honour was universally agreed among the heroes of old to be worse than death; that was the true defeat. 'A mæȝ ȝnornian se ðe nu fram þis piȝpleȝan þendan

þenceð ', said Byrhtwold. But to preserve honour and
fair fame, even at the cost of life, that was the best for
every man, as Beowulf observed (1387 f, 2664-6). The
poet of *Maldon* understood and emphasized the ascendancy
of spirit over the weakness of the body required by this
code. The heroic faith was that all was well with the man
whose spirit remained unyielding, however painfully the
body might be sacrificed. This principle has never been
more directly and clearly expressed than by Byrhtwold,
the *eald ʒeneat*, who taught courage in the words:

> Hiʒe sceal þe heardra, heorte þe cenre,
> mod sceal þe mare, þe ure mæʒen lytlað.

Not merely in clear understanding of the heroic code,
but in the restrained strength of its presentation of heroic
behaviour *Maldon* may be said to be the most heroic of
poems. It has all the concentration and dramatic interest
of the fierce and fiery Norse lays, and yet is not marred
by any tendency to exaggeration. Byrhtnoð does not
' die laughing ', as do some heroes in Norse poetry, anxious
to exhibit their heroism, but thanking God, as he lies
mortally wounded, for the joys of his life. Then follow the
heroic words of the retainers who will not leave the battle,
and every detail is true and real ; the conventionality of
their sentiments only makes them ring truer. The poet's
art in presenting these speeches is admirable : they are
varied and individual, but they recur always to the same
theme.

The poet shows restraint in his style as well as in his
representation of action. *Maldon* has less ornament than
any other Old English poem, and aims at severe simplicity
and directness. The traditional features of poetic style
are not absent, kennings and parallelism carried out in
the form of periphrasis, but in *Maldon* these devices are
used for emphasis rather than ornament. Even the undeniably rhetorical art of the retainers' speeches is little
more than plain statement of the heroic motives, adorned
only by metrical form and skilful sentence structure.

The verse of *Maldon* accordingly lacks the richness of *Beowulf* or of Cynewulf's poetry, but it is swifter, more forcible, and no less suitable for its purpose than the technically more ' correct ' verse of *Beowulf*. The theme of Byrhtnoð and his faithful retainers had no need of ornament.

Complaint has often been made of the ancient epic method followed in *Maldon*, by which the battle is described as a series of individual combats, feats and speeches. It is possibly true, as has been alleged, that the poet was not capable of giving a picture of the battle as a whole : the criticism is in any case irrelevant. The old method was undoubtedly the best one for the poet's purpose ; his real subject was not the battle, but the deeds and deaths of the English heroes. Like most of the old heroic poets, he was interested less in the spectacle and movements of battle than in the heroic problem and how it was solved by the hero. In so far as general description is introduced, it is only a background and a means of indicating how hard and stern was the situation to be faced. The speeches of the loyal retainers, rightly for the poet's purpose, occupy a much more prominent place than the noise and carnage ; we are not told how the vikings advanced, whether their wings enveloped the smaller body of English troops, but we are told in full of Byrhtnoð's exhortations, his skill in the front of battle, and his heroic death. These were the essential points for a poem on heroes, and especially for a poem on heroes in whom the poet and his audience had a personal interest.

It should be observed, too, that the individual action often has a symbolical significance, representing the action of many. Probably the young gallant who amused himself by hawking before the battle was only one of many who had strayed from the main body of the army. When Wulfstan and two others went to defend the ford, they must have had their men with them, but they are not mentioned ; nor is it credible that only one viking attempted to cross the ford and was killed. Only once (l. 282) does the poet state that others were acting in the same way, but often he clearly means to imply it.

Thus the material is selected and presented in the way that best suited the poet's purpose. It is unfortunate that a poem which shows so strong a sense of proportion, of the right place for every poetic stone in the main structure, has come down to us incomplete. To judge from the part of *Maldon* still extant, only *Beowulf* among Old English poems shows a superior sense of structure (cf above, p. 24) ; though similarly careful construction is evident also in some others—notably *Guðlac, Wanderer,* and *Deor.*

The verse technique of *Maldon* does not show the versatility and range of *Beowulf* or some of Cynewulf's poetry, but no such range is required. In *Maldon* nothing but strong progressive verse is needed, and this the poet is always able to produce. His verse does not always follow the strict rules formulated by Sievers from the practice of the older poets, but it should not be inferred from this that the verse is rough or prosaic. It has no relation to the doggerel school exemplified in many of the late poems of the Chronicle. There is indeed no other verse in Old English of such swift firm movement, or such fluency in transition from one half-line to the next. The customary caesura in the middle or at the end of the line practically disappears, when the division between half-lines falls between an auxiliary verb and its infinitive, as in 2, 6, 7, 9-10, 17, &c. The rhythm is usually definitely marked, and the number of syllables in the sinkings not excessive ; and these are the essential virtues in Old English metre. The frequent use of anacrusis, and occasional licences in the placing of the alliterative stave, do not affect the crispness and force of the rhythm. There is not a poetically weak passage in the whole poem.

The Battle of Maldon stands in the small and distinguished company of great poems composed on contemporary public events. *Maldon* must also be conceded the proud position of being the greatest battle-poem in the English language —or perhaps the only battle-poem in our language that can justly be called great ; and it has achieved greatness through being primarily not a poem of battle, but a poem of heroism.

THE OLD ENGLISH MANUSCRIPT (BURNED 1731)

The manuscript in which *The Battle of Maldon* was formerly preserved also contained among other matters the unique text of Asser's *Life of King Alfred* ; and something of its history is known through the attention which Asser's work attracted.[1] The manuscript once belonged to the antiquary John Leland, who died in 1552 ; later it was in the possession of Archbishop Parker, who published from it the text of Asser's *Life*. It was not to be found among Parker's manuscripts after his death, and thus did not go with the rest of his collection to Corpus Christi College, Cambridge. Somehow it had found its way into the library of Lord Lumley, where it was seen and described by Dr. Thomas James, Bodley's first librarian, in 1600. Early in the seventeenth century it had passed to the Cotton Library, where it remained until it was almost completely destroyed by fire in 1731. Only a few charred fragments survive, still kept in the British Museum under the old Cottonian pressmark, Otho A xii.

The volume at the time of the fire consisted of at least two originally separate manuscripts bound together. The various works contained in the complete volume are listed by Thomas Smith in his catalogue of the Cotton Library, published in 1696 ; they were : [2]

OTHO A xii

1. Asserius Menevensis de gestis Alfredi Regis, charactere antiquo.

2. Exorcismus superstitiosus adversus febres, Latine, præmissis & intermixtis Saxonicis.

---

[1] The information that can be extracted from notices and descriptions of the text of Asser has been set forth by W. H. Stevenson, *Asser's Life of King Alfred*, pp. xiii f.

[2] Smith, p. 67.

3. Fragmentum quoddam Historicum de Eadrico &c., Saxonice.[1]
4. Vita & passio S. Ælphegi, Archiepiscopi Cantuariensis & martyris, per Osbernum, Monachum Cantuariensem.
5. Translatio S. Ælphegi.
6. Vita S. Odonis, Cantuariensis Archiepiscopi, per Osbernum, Monachum Cantuariensem.

7. Ælmeri, Monachi Ecclesiæ Christi Cantuariensis, epistolæ, in quibus tractat de munditia cordis, de discretione judicii, de affabilitate in sermone, de amore liberalitatis, prosecutione justitiæ, vigore disciplinæ, doctrinæ studio, cura pauperum, & erga debiles vel mente vel corpore compassione ; de bono vitæ claustralis, cum meditationibus sacris, cujusmodi sunt excitatio mentis in inquisitione Dei, & querimonia absentia metus Dei. Liber asceticus & vere pius.

8. Passio undecim mille virginum, a Rogero, Fordonensi Monacho scripta, anno 1181.
9. Translatio S. Vulfhildis virginis.
10. Vita S. Bertini Abbatis.
11. Vita B. Vulfhildis virginis.
12. Excerpta de vita S. virginis Æthelburgæ.
13. De S. Erchenwaldo.

Actually, the whole of Asser's *Life* was not written *charactere antiquo*. This describes the first hand, of which a specimen is given in facsimile by Wise in his edition of Asser, opposite p. 137 [2] ; this hand wrote out the first eighty-eight chapters, and was assigned by Wanley to the year 1000 or 1001. The rest of the Asser text was written in Old English insular characters by several hands ; this portion was considered by many who had seen the manuscript to be distinctly later in date, but Wanley, the only authoritative palaeographer among them, says : ' Asser is not written by one hand, but by several, and much about the same time.' [3] The whole of the Asser text was therefore written, probably, in the early eleventh century.

[1] This is *The Battle of Maldon*. The name Eadric is taken from line 11, evidently the first proper name recognizable as such to Smith. The description of the text as ' fragmentum ', together with Wanley's ' fragmentum capite & calce mutilum, sex foliis constans ', indicates that the poem was already so incomplete at the end of the seventeenth century as when Elphinston copied it, c. 1724.

[2] Reproduced in W. H. Stevenson's edition, opposite p. xxxii.

[3] Wanley's letter replying to Wise's questions has been discovered by Mr. K. Sisam and is cited by him in the *Review of English Studies*, vii. (1931) 2.

The Asser text and the two following items, the charm and *Maldon*, have disappeared without leaving a legible trace, but fortunately parts of leaves belonging to items 4 and 5 can still be read, and the writing here, according to Dr. R. Flower, belongs to the eleventh century, but late rather than early in the century. His view, based entirely on palaeographical indications, that this writing is later, is clearly right, since Osbern's work was not produced until well on in the second half of the century. There is not enough left of any other texts in the manuscript to afford any evidence for palaeographical dating.

It is clear, however, that other items in Smith's list are distinctly later in date. Smith says, no doubt accurately, that Roger of Forde's *Passion of the 11000 Virgins* was composed in the year 1181 [1] ; and Ælmer's work also belongs to the twelfth century.

According to Dr. James, who saw the manuscript in 1600, the volume consisted of 107 leaves ' in the least folio or greater quarto ', and we learn from Elphinston's transcript of *Maldon* that the poem occupied folios 57a–62b. Each folio side contained about 27 lines of verse, as compared with nearly 25 a page in the *Beowulf* manuscript ; hence we suppose that the manuscript was slightly larger in format than the *Beowulf* manuscript. So it seems hardly possible, when the first three items occupied 62 folios of this size, that the remaining 45 could have accommodated the ten following items. The manuscript seen by James in Lord Lumley's library can have been only a portion of the volume catalogued by Smith. But how many of the items listed by Smith were to be found in this manuscript James writes of ? Considerations of space and date suggest that they were the first six. Forty-five folios would not be an unreasonable allowance

---

[1] Another work by Roger of Forde (Forde Abbey in Devonshire) was dedicated to Abbot Baldwin, who died in 1180. For brief notices of Roger's works see Leland, *Commentarii* ed. A. Hall, Oxford 1729, p. 230, and DNB.

for Osbern's three works. At least some of them must have belonged to the same manuscript as *Maldon*, to account for the 45 additional folios ; probably all three of them did. They form a unified group not likely to be divided between two manuscripts. It is in any case practically certain that the charm and *Maldon* stood between a text copied early in the eleventh century and others copied in the last half (or, more probably, the last quarter) of the century. The text of *Maldon* can accordingly be assigned to the eleventh century, and it is more naturally associated with the following easterly items than with the Asser text (see below, p. 39).

Good reasons have been adduced by W. H. Stevenson (*Asser*, p. xlvi) for believing that the Asser in this manuscript was the identical text used by Florence of Worcester. If this is correct, nothing in the manuscript could be later than the end of the eleventh century, and items 7 and 8 of Smith's list must be excluded. These two items with the following five have a certain unity of interest and subject-matter, and probably formed a complete independent manuscript, which at some time in the seventeenth century was bound up with the volume described by James. This second manuscript may have been written at Barking, since four of the works contained in it have a strong local association.[1]

The first manuscript, comprising items 1-6, belonged to the eleventh century and probably came from Worcester. There is no proof that it was written there, but the *Maldon* text has linguistically the appearance of being a western copy of an eastern original.

---

[1] Wulfhild was abbess of Barking in the reign of Eadgar ; St. Æðelburh was the first abbess (later the monastery was dedicated to her jointly with the Virgin Mary), and St. Erconwald her brother was the founder. Moreover, items 7-13 would in various ways form a volume of specially suitable reading for the nuns of Barking.

THE BATTLE OF MALDON

ELPHINSTON'S TRANSCRIPT AND HEARNE'S PRINT

Some years before the destruction (in 1731) of the Cotton manuscript containing *The Battle of Maldon*, a transcript of the poem was made from that manuscript by John Elphinston, under-keeper of the Cottonian library, for the antiquary Richard Graves (1677–1729) of Mickleton in Gloucestershire. Graves gave this transcript to his friend Thomas Hearne,[1] who entered the following note at the head of the front page : ' Oct. 19. 1725. Given me by Mr. Graves. Transcribed by Mr. John Elphinston, late Under-Keeper of the Cott. Library, the same that transcribed Heming's Chartulary that printed [*sic*].' [2] Elphinston's transcript was probably made not long before it was passed on to Hearne ; it appears to be later than his transcript of Heming's chartulary, which Hearne received from Graves in 1722. Yet there is no conclusive evidence on this point. Hearne printed Elphinston's text as an appendix to his edition of John of Glastonbury's Chronicle, with due acknowledgment to both Graves and Elphinston.[3] Later the transcript of *Maldon* was left by Hearne, together with his diary and collections of notes [4] and other transcripts, to one W. Bedford, who sold them to Dr Richard Rawlinson. Rawlinson died in 1755, and he bequeathed the Hearne papers to the Bodleian Library, where the transcript of *Maldon* has remained ever since, unnoticed by editors and students of the poem, until it was recently identified by Mr. N. R. Ker. Elphinston's transcript now occupies pages 7–12 of MS Rawlinson B. 203 ; it is bound

[1] Concise accounts of Graves and Hearne are given in DNB. Much of the correspondence between these two friends is recorded in *Hearne's Collections 1705–35*, ed. Doble, Salter, &c., 11 vols. Oxford Historical Society 1884–1918.

[2] *Hemingi Chartularium Ecclesiae Wigornensis*. ed. T. Hearne, Oxford 1723. This transcript of Heming's chartulary is still extant, being MS Rawlinson B. 445 in the Bodleian library.

[3] See Hearne's introduction, I. li (below, p. 63).

[4] The collections published by the Oxford Historical Society: see above.

together with a transcript of a calendar, also printed by Hearne in the appendix to John of Gloucester (II. 557), a letter to Hearne from Thomas Granger (dated Oct. 5, 1725), and a transcript of Latin letters from MS Cotton Cleopatra C. iv.

Elphinston in transcribing the Cotton text of *Maldon* evidently tried to reproduce its form in all detail. As in his copy of Heming's chartulary, he imitated the shapes of the Old English letters, and left parts of compound words separated when so written in his original ; he also imitated the old manuscript in writing the text in continuous form, not in verses, but reproducing the manuscript points, whch were mainly metrical pauses. He also gives us the sections and capitals of the old text. The usual Old English abbreviations are employed, 7 (*&* once) for *and, þ'* for *þæt, þoñ* for *þonne*, and a horizontal stroke over a vowel to represent a following nasal consonant. This stroke usually represents *m*, but four times (ll. 77, 79, 145, 233) *n*, a value which this sign has but rarely in extant Old English manuscripts. Elphinston also reproduced the accents of the old text, and he indicates the beginning of each folio side in the Cotton manuscript (except folios 59b and 61b, which he has neglected to mark), but he does not specify the precise word in the line beginning the folio side. His own pages (measuring about $11\frac{1}{2}$ inches by $7\frac{1}{2}$, with generous margins at the outer sides) contain about the same number of lines as the old manuscript, and it seems that he was consciously attempting to reproduce the pagination of the original ; his pages begin seven times where the pages of the old text began, and only three times on a different line. It is not certain, of course, that Elphinston began his pages with the same word as the corresponding page of the Cotton manuscript, but there is at least a probability that his reproduction of the original is as exact in this matter as in most other details.

Though Elphinston imitated the form of the Old English letters, his writing slopes in a characteristically modern style, and the general effect is far from Anglo-Saxon. His writing is usually clear, but the formation of the letters is more variable than in Old English manuscripts, and some of the extreme variants are ambiguous. Thus the *r* of *leofre* in l. 7 is not certain, and may be an *n*, though it is true that the resemblance to *r* is slightly closer ; the upright stroke of *p* in *pæs* 23 rises higher above the line than usual, and it is possible that *þæs* should be read ; *þ* and *p* are at times very similar, and the first letter in *pest* 97 is about as near to one as the other ; *u* in *luðe* 86 might perhaps be taken as an *a* with an open top, being nearly as unlike Elphinston's normal *u* as it is unlike his *a*.

Richard Graves in a letter to Hearne in which he refers to Elphinston's transcript of Heming's chartulary writes slightingly of Elphinston's accuracy as a copyist : ' I have herewith sent a copy of Heming's Chartulary . . . But the misfortune is, the Copy was taken by one that seems to be not well vers'd in these Matters, tho' I believe the Faults are not so many but that with a little trouble they might not be corrected.' [1] It is still possible, however, to test Elphinston's accuracy in this transcript, and the test shows that Graves had really no cause to grumble. Comparison of Elphinston's copy with his original, MS Cotton Tiberius A xiii, proves that Elphinston was a fairly accurate copyist.[2] Yet though he had some skill in reading Old English hands, he knew little about the language, and often misinterpreted ambiguously formed letters ; but his mistakes are usually obvious and easily corrected. In the text of *Maldon* the total number of errors that a just and careful criticism recognizes is not large, and of these not more than four or five can be ascribed to Elphinston's copying.

Hearne's print of Elphinston's transcript is remarkably accurate, and does not appear to be guilty of a single mis-

[1] *Hearne's Collections*, VII. 334, Feb. [28], 1721/2 (i.e. 1722).
[2] This may be demonstrated with less trouble by comparing Hearne's very accurate print of Elphinston's copy of Heming's chartulary with the charters printed by Kemble and Birch from MS Cotton Tiberius A xiii.

print. Such discrepancies as there are between Hearne's
text and Elphinston's copy have arisen from misreading of
Elphinston's writing, as in *huȝende* 122 and *ȝearo* 274 ; or
else are substitutions of equivalent symbols, as in *prǽce* 257,
lǽȝe 279, Ða 162, 202, 273, ða 277, and in various places
where one type of *s* is substituted for another ; or else
they are deliberate corrections, like *þā* in line 10. Occa-
sionally the grouping of letters in words or parts of words
differs, and twice this difference is due to Hearne's deliberate instruction to the printer : in 310 he has wrongly
divided Elphinston's *acpehte* into *ac pehte*, and *ealdȝeneat*
into *eald ȝeneat*—perhaps justifiably (see the textual note).

The printed text gives, inevitably, a different impression of certain details more accurately represented in
written form. Thus Hearne prints *p . . . . ȝe* in 10, with
the dots spaced wide apart, but in the transcript the dots
between *p* and *ȝ* are so close together that Elphinston can
not have meant to suggest that as many as four letters were
missing ; he leaves space for two. Similarly in . *.ulde*
33 so little space is left that any doubt about the generally accepted restoration *hilde* is finally removed. Again
in line 86 Hearne's print places *onȝunnon* a full line
below *fundon*, indicating a new section of the poem,
though it would be the only one not marked by a capital.
In the transcript *onȝunnon* and the following words in
the line are only slightly lower than *fundon*, and it
seems unlikely that Elphinston meant to indicate a new
section here. Better sense is obtained if no break in the
sentence is made at that point. It is especially in such
details that Elphinston's transcript is more valuable than
Hearne's print as a basis for an edition. Hearne's print
was as efficient a print as one could ask for, but it necessarily yields less information than the actual transcript.

THE HISTORY AND LINGUISTIC CHARACTER OF THE TEXT

The beginning and ending of the poem are lost, apparently, through loss of whole leaves from the Cotton manuscript at some time before 1696, when Smith described it (above, p. 30). How much of the poem is missing it is impossible to determine, as we have no exact idea of its original scope. It seems likely, however, that less has been lost at the end than at the beginning, perhaps one leaf (about 56 lines) at the end, and two or three at the beginning.

Nothing very definite can be made out about the history of the text. Though we should expect the poem to be composed in Essex, the language of the text as we have it is mainly late West Saxon. The non-West Saxon forms are few, and those which can be pronounced to be characteristically eastern extremely rare. Almost the only certainly eastern form is one which editors have always removed—*gofol* in line 61 (see the textual note). A probable south-eastern ' reverse ' spelling with *y* for *e* is *stynt* 51. The confusion of *æ* and *e* in stressed syllables is common in south-eastern texts, but at the late date of the manuscript (end of the eleventh century), it may be the beginning of the general process of replacing *æ* graphically by *e*. The forms showing this confusion are : *easteðe* 63 (cf *stæðe* 25), *leʒ*, p.t. 276 (elsewhere *læʒ*), *prec*, p.t. 279 ; and with *æ* for *e* : *pælræste* 113, *stædefæste* 127. The general absence of the rounding of accented *a* before nasal consonants (the rounded *o* occurs only in *formoni* 239) is eastern rather than western ; but as such rounding is absent over an extended area, it provides no precise evidence of dialect.

The language of *The Battle of Maldon* is in the main so consistently and characteristically West Saxon that it is difficult to avoid the conclusion that the text is in some way connected with the south-west. While West Saxon influence was, undeniably, widespread in the eleventh century, and originally West Saxon characteristics then appear in documents written in various parts of England, there are some forms in *Maldon* which are known only in texts from the south-west or west. One of the most definitely western is *syllan* ' to hand over ' in 38, 46, and its subjunctive *syllon* in 61, together with *sylfra*, 38 (see Luick § 282). South-western also is *hremmas* ' ravens ' in 106 (= *hræfnas*). Of many other forms, such as those containing normal late West Saxon *y*, *ʒystas* 86, *fynd* 82, *scype* 40, *sy* 215, it can be said that although a certain proportion of them would not necessarily at this date indicate a western scribe, the consistency of their occurrence in *Maldon* does point in that direction.

We have seen already (above, p. 33) that an independent piece of evidence associates the *Maldon* manuscript with Worcester ; and the linguistic character of the extant text might well have been acquired in that locality. The idea becomes still more plausible when we recall that in the late eleventh century, when the manuscript was completed, Worcester was one of the chief centres in England where Old English literature was still read and copied.

But though the copy is western, the version copied, we believe, was eastern, and the exemplar probably did not antedate the copy by many years. *Maldon* may well have been brought to the west together with the other eastern texts following it in the manuscript, and these (by Osbern) had only recently been written. Moreover, the easternism *ʒofol* in line 61 appears to be a late eastern form, one that is first known in the tenth century.

The previous history of the text in the east is unknown. One guess about it can be made, however. Though the text is metrically fairly sound, the irregularities which do occur (such as the unnecessary misplacing of the alliterating word in lines 45*b* and 75*b*, and other cases of interference with the order of the words) are such as would arise most easily in oral transmission. We conjecture that the poem was preserved orally for a time, and the account of Byrht-noð and his last battle in *Liber Eliensis* is the final echo of this oral tradition ; then a written copy was made

4   39

while the poem continued to be transmitted orally; a late eastern copy was brought to Worcester towards the end of the eleventh century and there transcribed, with consistent westernizing of the word forms, into a manuscript already containing a copy of Asser's life of Alfred.

A NOTE ON THE EDITED TEXT

The Battle of Maldon is here edited from Elphinston's transcript in MS Rawlinson B 203 (designated E), which reproduces most features of the text as it stood in the eleventh-century Cotton MS Otho A xii (burned in 1731; see above, p. 34 f). In the present edition the text has been arranged in long lines, and has been punctuated in accordance with modern usage. The abbreviations of the transcript have been expanded without notice, except that instances of a horizontal stroke over a vowel used to represent a following *n* are recorded among the textual variants. The main sections of the poem are marked in the transcript by capitals (usually large capitals) and indentation at the margin; these main sections occur at lines 17, 62, 68, 130, 162, 202 and 273. Subsections are marked in the transcript by capitals alone, usually small capitals; these subsections appear in the edited text as paragraphs, but the beginning is less deeply indented than at the main sections. A few of the smaller capitals cannot be regarded as marking subsections and are ignored; these occur in: Byrhtnoð 101, Stihte 127, Him 152, Nu 175, 215, Ic 246. Once (at line 25) a paragraph is made where there is no indication in the transcript. Otherwise the paragraphing follows strictly the capitalization in Elphinston's transcript. In the textual variants page-references are to E, folio references to (the burned) MS Cotton Otho A xii.

THE BATTLE OF MALDON

(*Bodleian Library, MS Rawlinson B. 203, pp. 7–12*)

brocen purde.
Het þa hyssa hpæne hors forlætan,
feor afysan 7 forð ӡanӡan,
hicӡan to handum 7 to hiӡe ӡodum.
Þa þæt Offan mæӡ ærest onfunde,   5

---

2 *hors forlætan :* horses were used by OE forces mainly for
movement and transport and not often in battle, though there is
evidence of OE cavalry in the eleventh century, in ASC and the
ON account of the battle of Stamford Bridge.   The driving away
of the horses was a gesture indicating not only that there was
serious fighting on hand, but that there was no intention of fleeing
from the spot.   The tradition of dismounting for battle and sending
away the horses lasted long.   Miss Ashdown quotes an example
from Laӡamon's *Brut* and an especially near parallel from the much
later ballad of Otterburn.

3 *feor afysan :* ' drive (the horses) afar '.   This is better than
taking *afysan* in its intransitive sense : ' hasten afar ' would be
an unnatural order to the army, even if it is assumed that the
advance to the battlefield is described here.   More probably the
English are already by the Blackwater, and Byrhtnoð now wishes
to array his men in position.

4 *hicӡan to handum :* though *hicӡan to* can mean ' to trust in '
—and some editors so interpret it here—the parallel uses (below
ll. 123, 128, *Finnesburh* 11, *Exodus* 218, *Psalm* 77[20]) support the
more generally accepted interpretation ' to be intent upon '.

5 *Offan mæӡ :* Offa was one of Byrhtnoð's chief followers, as
is evident from his comment at the meeting, ll. 198 f, but his rank
and descent are not known.   His kinsman here is a young man
(*cniht* 9), who was amusing himself by hawking on the bank of the
Blackwater estuary.   This may have been partly a gesture of
bravado to show his indifference to the enemy.   Byrhtnoð evidently
shows disapproval of such lack of discipline (*yrhðo* 6) and gives
the order to dismount, so that all shall be ready for battle.   The
young gallant can hardly be identical with the kinsman of Offa
named Gadd in 287 ; the kinsman named at that point must have
been a senior and well-known man.

5 *ærest* is probably used idiomatically to give a sense of immediacy

41

þæt se eorl nolde yrhðo ᵹeþolian,
he let him þa of handon leofne fleoᵹan
hafoc wið þæs holtes 7 to þære hilde stop.
Be þam man mihte oncnapan þæt se cniht nolde
pacian æt þam piᵹᵹe, þa he to pæpnum fenᵹ.   10
Eac him polde Eadric his ealdre ᵹelæstan,
frean to ᵹefeohte ; onᵹan þa forð beran
ᵹar to ᵹuþe. He hæfde ᵹod ᵹeþanc
þa hpile þe he mid handum healdan mihte
bord 7 brad spurd : beot he ᵹelæste   15

7 leofne : leofre *E* (*see p.* 36).   10 piᵹᵹe : p....ᵹe *E* (*see p.* 37) ;
þam : þ'ā *E*, þā *H*.

---

to the temporal conj. *þa*, so that *þa..ærest onfunde* may be rendered
'upon perceiving'. Cf the similar use of *ærest* in *Beowulf* 6, where
recognition of the idiom shows that the *syððan ærest* clause must
be construed with the following lines ; Scyld could not become a
conqueror while still an infant. Cf also *Crist* 1151. Yet it is possible also that *þa* is here the adv. 'then', and that l. 7 begins a
new sentence. The punctuation and interpretation adopted here
seem more in keeping with the word-order (cf. 25, 181, 202, 285,
295) and with the rapid fluent movement of the poem at this point.

6 *se eorl :* Byrhtnoð, who is called 'earl' in the sense of the word
derived from Scandinavian *jarl*, a noble of highest rank, an under-
king. In this sense *eorl* is synonymous with OE *ealdormann*,
and Byrhtnoð is elsewhere (as in ASC) given the title of *ealdormann*.
The title *eorl* at this time was given to the ruler of one of the greater
divisions of England, as Northumbria, and was at first used only
in the districts where Scandinavian rulers had been in authority,
but was later extended to the rest of England. Before Scandinavian
influence altered the sense of the word, *eorl* was used of the aristocratic followers of a king or chief, such men as Ælfwine and most
of the followers of Byrhtnoð mentioned by name in this poem.
See further 51 n.

8 *holtes :* the nearest point of wooded ground would be around
Hazeleigh, behind the English position. This was an offshoot of
the large Dansbury forest lying west and south-west of Maldon.

10 *piᵹᵹe :* the late spelling with *iᵹ* for *ī* fits the space indicated
by E's p....ᵹe better than the normal *piᵹe*. See p. 37.

12 *onᵹan :* auxiliary of past tense, used of completed action which
was a process rather than a simple act : it is thus quite different
from modern inceptive 'began to', and is more nearly equivalent
to 'proceeded to' with the implication 'and actually did'.

14–15 *þe hpile...spurd :* the use of this formula implies that Eadric

þa he ætforan his frean feohtan sceolde.

Ða þær Byrhtnoð onᵹan beornas trymian,
rad 7 rædde, rincum tæhte
hu hi sceoldon standan 7 þone stede healdan,
7 bæd þæt hyra randas rihte heoldon   20
fæste mid folman 7 ne forhtedon na.
Þa he hæfde þæt folc fæᵹere ᵹetrymmed,
he lihte þa mid leodon þær him leofost pæs,
þær he his heorðperod holdost piste.

Þa stod on stæðe, stiðlice clypode   25
picinᵹa ar, pordum mælde,
se on beot abead brimliþendra

20 randas : randan E 26 ar begins p. 7b, fol. 57b.

---

subsequently met his death in the fight ; so also in 83. (B. S.
Phillpotts, MLR xxiv. 174.)

17 f. There is a distinction implied between the men of the
fyrd, the men of the district who are called together in time of
war, and the men of Byrhtnoð's own household, the heorðperod of
l. 24. Byrhtnoð instructs the men of the fyrd, riding along their
ranks, showing them where to stand, and the position which they
must strive to defend ; and he exhorts them to hold the shield-wall
firm. Then he dismounts among those of his personal following
who are his closest associates (ll. 23–4).

20 heoldon : subjunctive, with late confusion of -on with the
normal subjunctive plural ending -en ; similar pl.subjs. in -on
are forhtedon 21, forᵹyldon 32, dælon 33, ᵹanᵹon 56, syllon 61,
&c.

20 randan is almost certainly a copyist's error, as no weak form
of the noun is known elsewhere, and among the many forms in
ll. 19 and 20 ending in -an the error is natural.

26 mælde : not a Norse word, despite Björkman (Scand. Loan-
words, p. 104) ; the same traditional half-line is found in poems
composed before the Scandinavian settlements (Elene 351, Andreas
300, Genesis 2912). Björkman's notion was based on the erroneous
assumption that loss of þ before l as in mælan did not occur in
Anglian ; but cf (ᵹe)stælan in Beowulf, Guthlac and Cynewulf's
poems, several times where the longer staðelian would be metrically
unsuitable. And there are still more Anglian instances.

27 on beot : all translators render this ' boastfully ', though the
viking messenger does not boast, but threatens, being less concerned
about glory than about blackmail. ' Threat ' is the common sense
of beot (BT, s.v.) and ' threateningly ' suits the context here. Cf

ærænde to þam eorle þær he on ofre stod :
' Me sendon to þe sæmen snelle,
heton ðe secʒan þæt þu most sendan raðe   30
beaʒas wið ʒebeorʒe, 7 eop betere is
þæt ʒe þisne ʒarræs mid ʒafole forʒyldon
þonne pe spa hearde hilde dælon.
Ne þurfe pe us spillan, ʒif ʒe spedaþ to þam ;

33 þonne : þon *E* ; hilde : ..ulde *E* (*see p.* 37).

Ælfric, *Lives of the Saints* (ed. Skeat) II. 316/43 : *Hinʒuar sende to þam cyninʒe* [*Eadmunde*] *beotlic ærende* ' a threatening message '.

29 f. In this speech the sg. pronoun of the second person alternates with the pl. There seems to be no difficulty in taking the sg. as applying specifically to Byrhtnoð and the pl. to the English generally. In 34 the pl. is used because Byrhtnoð alone would not be expected to make the payment ; usually the money for paying off the Danes was raised in the form of a tax on the various landholders. In 36 the sg. is used because Byrhtnoð alone is assumed to have the decision in his hands.

30 *most :* context makes the sense ' must ' probable, instead of the more usual ' may '. This sense is old, being found in *Beowulf* 2886, &c. There is no reason to suppose (with B. S. Phillpotts, MLR xxiv. 188) that there is any confusion of *mæʒ* and *mot* due to Scandinavian influence.

32 The ʒ's in this line do not all alliterate together ; the two palatal ʒ's alliterate together and the two velar ʒ's, so that we have an example of double alliteration ; other examples of the same pattern *abba* occur in 34, 50, 159, 189, 314. The two kinds of ʒ did not alliterate with each other in this poem ; *ʒramum* in 100 and *onʒan* in 265 have no part in the alliteration. Double alliteration also occurs in the pattern *abab* in 24, 63, 68, 98, 255, 285, 318, 320, &c.

33 *þonne :* E's *þon* is a known form, but it is so rare that it seems more likely that E or an earlier copyist overlooked the mark of abbreviation over the *n* of *þoñ* = *þonne. hearde* goes with *hilde* rather than with *pe* : *heard* is the common epithet of battle (as in l. 214, *Elene* 83, &c.), whereas such an expression as *pe spa hearde* would be difficult to parallel. Translate the line : ' Than that we should join in bitter conflict.'

34 *spedaþ to þam :* the idiom is not found elsewhere, and the precise sense is not certain. The most natural sense would be : ' if you are prosperous to that extent ', i.e. if you are wealthy enough to meet our demand. Similarly Skeat : ' if you are good

ꝥe pillað pið þam ȝolde ȝrið fæstnian.   35
Ȝyf þu þæt ȝerædest þe her ricost eart,
þæt þu þine leoda lysan pille,
syllan sæmannum on hyra sylfra dom
feoh pið freode 7 niman frið æt us,
ꝥe pillaþ mid þam sceattum us to scype ȝanȝan,   40
on flot feran 7 eop friþes healdan.'
  Byrhtnoð maþelode, bord hafenode,
pand pacne æsc, pordum mælde,
yrre 7 anræd aȝeaf him andspare :
' Ȝehyrst þu, sælida, hpæt þis folc seȝeð ?   45
Hi pillað eop to ȝafole ȝaras syllan,
ættrynne ord 7 ealde spurd,

36 þæt: þat E.   38 syllan : syllán E.

---

for the amount demanded.' BT has : ' if you succeed in doing this.'

35 *ȝrið* : less general in sense than *frið* in 39 and 41. *ȝrið* was truce or protection from hostility within definite conditions ; *frið* was ' peace ' in general. *ȝrið* is one of the few Scandinavian words in the poem ; the others are *æsc(here)* 69 and *drenȝ* 149 ; but cf also *eorl* 6 n, *ceallian* 91 n and *mælan* 26 n.

42 *bord hafenode* : *hafenian* means ' lift up ' rather than ' grasp ', as many previous editors have rendered the word ; see NED, s.v. *heven* v.¹. The raising of the shield was a sign that an announcement was to be made. Similarly in *Exodus* 252 f the herald (*hilde-calla*) ran out in front of the host and *bord up ahof* to obtain silence for his speech. So also do Leofsunu in 244 and Byrhtwold in 309, and the brandishing of the spear is apparently another gesture appealing for attention in 236, 255, 310. This speech-making in battle was a reality, not a poetic convention.

45 In the second half-line it is the second lift (*seȝeð*) that alliter-ates ; so also in 75 and 288. The metre could be regularized by inversion here and in 75, but hardly in 288.

47 *ættrynne ord 7 ealde spurd* : *ord* is clearly sing., as the form of its modifying adj. shows, but *spurd* is more probably plural, like *ȝaras* in the preceding line. If *spurd* is singular, *ealde* must be taken as a ' poetic ' use of the weak adjective, unique in this poem and unparalleled in the known late OE poems. *ord* is a generic singular, ' deadly point (of spears) ', but *spurd* is strictly parallel to *ȝaras*. *ealde* used of swords and weapons implies excel-lence and trustworthiness. In OE poetry the best weapons are old heirlooms ; cf *Beowulf* 795, 1458, 2563, 2682, &c.

þa hereзeatu þe eop æt hilde ne deah.
Brimmanna boda, abeod eft onзean,
seзe þinum leodum miccle laþre spell,   50
þæt her stynt unforcuð eorl mid his perode
þe pile зealзean eþel þysne,
Æþelredes eard, ealdres mines
folc 7 foldan. Feallan sceolon
hæþene æt hilde. To heanlic me þinceð   55
þæt зe mid urum sceattum to scype зanзon
unbefohtene, nu зe þus feor hider

55–6 ceð *in* þinceð . . . scype *begins fol.* 58a.   56 зanзon *begins
p.* 8a.

---

48 *þa hereзeatu :* C. Brett points out in MLR xxii. 260 that
hereзeatu has more significance in this passage if it has something
of its legal sense : ' a feudal service originally consisting of weapons,
horses and other military equipments, restored to a lord on the
death of his tenant '. Byrhtnoð proposes to pay tribute in weapons,
as in a heriot, but it will be a heriot that will not profit those who
exact it. The singular form of the word as well as the context
supports Brett's suggestion ; the word is normally used in the
plural, and is not otherwise recorded in the singular, except in legal
use. This double-edged use of the word is characteristic of the
grim irony of Byrhtnoð's whole answer.

51 *unforcuð eorl :* a traditional phrase ; cf *Andreas* 475, 1263
eorl unforcuð, where *unforcuð* seems to mean primarily ' dauntless ',
though there may be some connotation of nobility as well. *eorl*
here probably has something of its older meaning ' noble warrior '
from association with the traditional phrase.

52 *зealзean :* altered by most editors to *зeealзian*. Probably,
however, *зealзean* represents the late pronunciation of *ealзian*, with
a з-sound developed initially (cf Sievers, § 212, note 2 ; though
such forms are not confined to Kent). The early texts never have
the initial з- or зe- in this word, nor is it logical to add зe- to this
naturally perfective verb. It may be doubted whether *зeealзian*
had any genuine existence : apparent examples (see BT supplement)
occur in manuscripts notorious for their inaccurate use of зe- (see
Schröer, *Ben. Rule* xliii). The alliteration in this line shows that
the original text had *ealзian* or *alзian*, not *зealзean*.

57 *nu зe þus feor,* &c. : this gives the sentence an ironic turn ;
it would be a shame for the vikings to take their spoil without a
fight, since they have troubled to come so far for the encounter :
see F. Klaeber, Anglia liii. 227.

on urne eard in becomon.

Ne sceole ȝe spa softe sinc ȝeȝanȝan :
us sceal ord 7 ecȝ ær ȝeseman,   60
ȝrim ȝuðpleȝa, ær þe ȝofol syllon.'

Het þa bord beran, beornas ȝanȝan
þæt hi on þam eásteðe ealle stodon.

Ne mihte þær for pætere perod to þam oðrum :
þær com flopende flod æfter ebban ;   65
lucon laȝustreamas. To lanȝ hit him þuhte
hpænne hi toȝædere ȝaras beron.

Hi þær Pantan stream mid prasse bestodon,
Eastseaxena ord 7 se æschere ;
ne mihte hyra æniȝ oþrum derian,   70
buton hpa þurh flanes flyht fyl ȝename.

Se flod ut ȝepat. þa flotan stodon ȝearope,
picinȝa fela piȝes ȝeorne.
Het þa hæleða hleo healdan þa bricȝe

61 pe : þe *E.*

---

61 *ȝofol* has been unanimously emended to *ȝafol* by previous
editors, but *ȝofol* should stand. Miss F. E. Harmer points out that
ȝofol occurs twice in the will of Æðelwyrd (BCS 1010), who owned
land at Ickham near Canterbury. This will, dating probably from
958, is an original and its dialect is Kentish. In ME the change
of *af* to *of* belongs to Essex and the East Midlands : cf the forms
cited by Morsbach, *Mittelenglische Grammatik*, § 87, note 4, and the
frequent occurrence of *gouel* in *Genesis and Exodus*, and dative
goule beside *gavele* in *Vices and Virtues*.

66 *lucon laȝustreamas* : Laborde's explanation (*Eng. Hist. Review :*
see p. 3–4) of this expression is plausible : the incoming tide flows
up the channels of the Blackwater around Northey island, where
the vikings are, and its two streams meet at the western end of
the island. Others have taken the phrase to mean that the incoming tide met and mingled with the current of the river. This
is possible, but less pointed. *lucon* might also mean ' enclosed ',
in that the tidal stream prevented the vikings from crossing. The
absolute use of *lucan* in this sense is however less natural than that
assumed in the first interpretation.

69 *æschere* : the *here* or raiding force from the *æscas*, distinctively
Scandinavian ships built of ash wood. The OE word is an angliciz-
ing of ON *askr*. The *askr* was the usual viking warship : see
H. Falk, *Altnordisches Seewesen*, p. 87.

piȝan piȝheardne—se pæs haten Þulfstan—   75
cafne mid his cynne : þæt pæs Ceolan sunu,
þe ðone forman man mid his francan ofsceat
þe þær baldlicost on þa bricȝe stop.
Þær stodon mid Þulfstane piȝan unforhte,
Ælfere 7 Maccus, modiȝe tpeȝen,   80
þa noldon æt þam forda fleam ȝepyrcan,
ac hi fæstlice pið ða fynd peredon
þa hpile þe hi pæpna pealdan moston.
Þa hi þæt onȝeaton 7 ȝeorne ȝesapon,
þæt hi þær bricȝpeardas bitere fundon,   85
onȝunnon lyteȝian þa laðe ȝystas,

77 francan: francā E.   79 Þulfstane: pulfstāe E.   81 fleam
begins p. 8b, fol. 58b.   86 laðe: luðe E (*see p.* 36).

---

75 Wulfstan owned the land at Purleigh (OE *Purlea*), just south
of Maldon, and had other estates not far distant. Napier and
Stevenson offer the opinion that ' it was probably this local connexion that caused Byrhtnoð to select Wulfstan to guard the
bridge ' (*Crawford Ch.* p. 123). The land in the parish of St. Mary
Maldon which now lies between Purleigh and the estuary is not
given as a separate possession in Domesday Book, so that it is
even likely that it was Wulfstan's land that the English force was
standing on and defending.

76 *cafne mid his cynne :* ' valiant as was the stock from which
he sprang ' or ' come of a valiant stock ', a variant of *heardes cynnes*
in 266. Wulfstan was possibly related to Byrhtnoð himself : see
below, p. 85.

77 *francan :* etymologically ' the Frankish spear ', and originally
referring, probably, to the barbed spear said by Agathias to be
favoured by the Franks ; such spears are found both in Anglo-
Saxon and Frankish graves, and Gildas speaks of the *uncinata tela*
of the English invaders. But *franca* came also to be used as a
general term for ' spear ', just as was *ȝar* (properly the spear with
wedge-shaped head derived from the Celts in the early iron age) :
in 138 and 140 the same weapon is called *franca* and *ȝar*. In 77
the *franca* is thrown, but in 140 the verb *stanȝ* implies that Byrhtnoð
thrust it into his adversary. If the term has a specialized sense
there it probably refers to the thrusting spear with very long (often
3 feet or more) socket and barbed head, used for piercing the enemy
shield and pulling it down ; the long socket prevented the enemy
from hewing the head off.

bædon þæt hi upȝanȝ aȝan moston,
ofer þone ford faran, feþan lædan.

Ða se eorl onȝan for his ofermode
alyfan landes to fela laþere ðeode ;   90
onȝan ceallian þa ofer cald pæter
Byrhtelmes bearn—beornas ȝehlyston :
' Nu eop is ȝerymed : ȝað ricene to us
ȝuman to ȝuþe. Ȝod ana pat
hpa þære pælstope pealdan mote.'   95

Þodon þa pælpulfas, for pætere ne murnon,
picinȝa perod ; pest ofer Pantan
ofer scir pæter scyldas peȝon,
lidmen to lande linde bæron.
Þær onȝean ȝramum ȝearope stodon   100
Byrhtnoð mid beornum. He mid bordum het
pyrcan þone pihaȝan 7 þæt perod healdan

87 upȝanȝ : upȝanȝan E. 97 pest : pest E (see p. 36).

---

87 *upȝanȝ : upȝanȝan* in E is probably a copyist's error, as no
weak form of this word is known elsewhere in OE, and in the suc-
cession *upȝanȝ aȝan* the addition of *-an* would be a familiar type
of error. Cf *randan* in l. 20.

91 *ceallian ofer cald pæter :* the traditional association of *cald* in
the sense ' ill-omened ' or ' baleful ' with verbs of calling suggests
that in this passage the waters of the Pante are not only ' cold '
in the literal sense, but also ' fateful ' : cf *The Address of the Soul
to the Body* 15 : *cleopað þonne spa cearful caldan reorde ;* and
Atlakviða 2/3 : *hallaði þú Knéfrøðr kaldri roddu. ceallian* is usually
regarded as the first occurrence in English of the Norse word *kalla,*
but this is at least to be doubted. The sense here corresponds
closely with that of the native English noun *hildecalla* ' herald in
battle ', and *ceallian* may be a survival of an old poetic word that
had fallen out of colloquial use, until restored by the wide adoption
of *callen* from ON *kalla* in ME.

92 *beornas ȝehlyston :* the men on both sides were silent so that
Byrhtnoð's reply might be heard.

98 *scir pæter : scir* applied to water usually means ' clear ', but the
waters of the Blackwater are dull and muddy. Still or slow-moving
water, however, reflects light even more readily when muddy than
clear, and the epithet probably refers to this surface sheen. *scirpæter*
' water forming a boundary ' is not very likely in the context.

102 *pihaȝan :* this is the same as the *scyldburh* in 242 and the
bordhaȝa of *Elene* 652 and the *scildpeall* of *Beowulf* 3118. The

fæste pið feondum. Þa pæs feohte neh,
tir æt ʒetohte. Þæs seo tid cumen
þæt þær fæʒe men feallan sceoldon.　　　　105
Þær pearð hream ahafen. Hremmas pundon,
earn æses ʒeorn. Þæs on eorþan cyrm.
Hi leton þa of folman feolhearde speru,
ʒrimme ʒeʒrundene ʒaras fleoʒan.
Boʒan pæron bysiʒe, bord ord onfenʒ.　　　　110
Biter pæs se beaduræs. Beornas feollon
on ʒehpæðere hand, hyssas laʒon.
Þund pearð Þulfmær, pælræste ʒeceas

103 feohte : fohte *E*.　107 ʒeorn *begins p. 9a*.　108 ras *in* ʒaras
begins fol. 59a.　109 ʒrimme *supplied*.　113 pearð : peard *E*.

---

pihaʒa was a defensive formation made by ranks of men placed
closely one behind another and holding their shields side by side
and overlapping so as to present a continuous wall. The front
rank of men held their shields before their breasts and the ranks
behind held theirs over their heads to protect both those in front
and themselves. This formation probably was from common
Germanic tradition : cf ON *skjaldborg, skjaldhagi*, OHG *sciltburg*.
See also A. S. Cook's *Judith*, l. 305 n.

108 *feolhearde* : ' hard as a file ' rather than ' sharpened by the
file ', as has also been suggested. The file was used to test the
temper of the blade : see Falk, *Altnordische Waffenkunde*, p. 20,
and cf ON *hneitir þél harðari* ' sword harder than a file ', cited
by Dame Bertha Phillpotts, *loc. cit.*

109 *ʒrimme ʒeʒrundene* : *ʒrimme* is added as an emendation.
ʒeʒrundene alone can not make a complete half-line, and it is evident
that a word has fallen out of the text. *ʒrimme* is supplied as the
only word to be found which alliterates and makes sense in the
context. It completes a phrase well attested in alliterative poetry :
cf *Ruin* 14 *ʒrimme ʒeʒrunden*, and in ME, *Pearl* 654 *þe glayue so
grymly grounde, Amis and Amiloun* 1353 *his grimly gare*, and the
whole phrase in *Sir Isumbras* 452 *with grymly growndyne gare.*

113 *pearð* : E's *peard*, and *pærd* for *pearð* in 116, may not be
scribal errors in the ordinary sense, as they are possibly very late
forms substituted by the copyist for *pearð* in his original. Such
forms as *pærd* and *pard* are well attested in the twelfth century,
but in OE past singular forms ending in *d* are so rare that the
instances are all regarded as scribal errors. Even at the end of
the eleventh century such forms are doubtful, and they are accordingly normalized here.

Byrhtnoðes mæʒ : he mid billum pearð,
his spustersunu, spiðe forheapen.   115
Þær pearð picinʒum piþerlean aʒyfen :
ʒehyrde ic þæt Eadpeard anne sloʒe
spiðe mid his spurde, spenʒes ne pyrnde,
þæt him æt fotum feoll fæʒe cempa ;
þæs him his ðeoden þanc ʒesæde   120
þam burþene, þa he byre hæfde.

Spa stemnetton stiðhicʒende
hysas æt hilde, hoʒodon ʒeorne
hpa þær mid orde ærost mihte
on fæʒean men feorh ʒepinnan,   125
piʒan mid pæpnum. Þæl feol on eorðan.
Stodon stædefæste, stihte hi Byrhtnoð,
bæd þæt hyssa ʒehpylc hoʒode to piʒe,
þe on Denon polde dom ʒefeohtan.

Þod þa piʒes heard, pæpen up áhof,   130
bord to ʒebeorʒe, 7 pið þæs beornes stop.
Eode spa anræd eorl to þam ceorle :
æʒþer hyra oðrum yfeles hoʒode.

116 pearð : pærd *E.*   122 stiðhicʒende : stið hicʒende *E,* stið
huʒende *H.*

---

115 *his spustersunu :* his sister's. son, whose death would be
specially grievous to Byrhtnoð.   There was everywhere in the
Germanic world a close bond between the uncle and his sister's
son, constantly referred to in the old literature ; it is first remarked
upon by Tacitus, *Germania* no i *sororum jiliis idem apud avunculum
qui apud patrem honor.   quidam sanctiorem artioremque hunc nexum
sanguinis arbitrantur et in accipiendis obsidibus magis exigunt.*

122 *stemnetton :* found only here in OE, but in ME compare
Saint Katherine (ed. Einenkel) 1265 : *Hwi studgi ʒe nu 7 steuentið
se stille ?*   Here *steuentið se stille* renders Latin *ommutescitis.*   The
ME ending *-ið* descends from OE *-iað* of the second class of weak
verbs, but the OE verbs in *-ettan* were always reformed in this
way in the ' Katherine ' group of texts, as in *leitin* from OE *leʒettan.*
The beginning of the process can be seen already in the Vespasian
Psalter : see C. Grimm's *Glossar* sub *ondettan.*   There can therefore
be no doubt that the verb in *Saint Katherine* represents an OE
stefnettan and is the same word as *stemnettan* here, and the ME
sense supports the gloss ' stand firm ' assigned by Sweet.

Sende ða se særinc suþerne ȝar
þæt ȝepundod pearð piȝena hlaford.   135
He sceaf þa mid ðam scylde þæt se sceaft tobærst,
7 þæt spere sprenȝde þæt hit spranȝ onȝean.
Ȝeȝremod pearð se ȝuðrinc : he mid ȝare stanȝ
plancne picinȝ þe him þa punde forȝeaf.
Frod pæs se fyrdrinc ; he let his francan padan   140
þurh ðæs hysses hals, hand pisode
þæt he on þam færsceaðan feorh ȝeræhte.

Ða he oþerne ofstlice sceat
þæt seo byrne tobærst : he pæs on breostum pund
þurh ða hrinȝlocan ; him æt heortan stod   145
ætterne ord. Se eorl pæs þe bliþra :
hloh þa modi man, sæde Metode þanc.

136 se *begins p. 9b* ; *fol. 59b is not recorded, but probably begins*
here.   145 hrinȝlocan : hrinȝ locā *E.*

---

134 *suþerne ȝar :* usually translated (though not by W. P. Ker
or M. Ashdown) as ' spear (thrown) from the south '—a very dubious
use of *suþerne,* and inadmissible in this context. This mistrans-
lation, which was taken to indicate that the vikings were on the
south side of the river (in spite of l. 97) influenced Freeman in his
erroneous identification of the battlefield. In reality the *suþerne
ȝar* was a spear of southern make ; weapons made in England and
France were favoured by the vikings ; cf the Norse poem on the
battle of Hafrsfjorðr :

      Hlaðnir váru holða   ok hvítra skjalda,
      vigra vestrœnna   ok valskra sverða.

' (The ships) were laden with fighting-men and white shields, spears
from the west and swords from France '. See also H. Falk,
Altnordische Waffenkunde, p. 40.

137 *he* (Byrhtnoð) is the subject of *sprenȝde* ; Byrhtnoð knocked
with the edge of his shield the spear that had struck him so that
the shaft broke and the spear-head fell away from him. Similar
movements of the shield that break the hostile weapon or send it
flying away are described in the sagas : see H. Falk, *Altnordische
Waffenkunde,* p. 149.

143 *oþerne :* sc. *færsceaðan* rather than *francan.*

146 *ætterne :* the usual form of this adj. is *ættren,* and the final *-e*
has been added probably on the analogy of the adjs. ending in
-erne. Other instances of the form *ætterne* in late OE are recorded
in BT Supplement.

ðæs dæȝpeorces þe him Drihten forȝeaf.

Forlet þa drenȝa sum daroð of handa
fleoȝan of folman, þæt se to forð ȝepat   150
þurh ðone æþelan Æþelredes þeȝen.
Him be healfe stod hyse únpeaxen,
cniht on ȝecampe, se full caflice
bræd of þam beorne blodiȝne ȝar,
Pulfstanes bearn, Pulfmær se ȝeonȝa ;   155
forlet forheardne faran eft onȝean.
Ord in ȝepod, þæt se on eorþan læȝ
þe his þeoden ær þearle ȝeræhte.
Eode þa ȝesyrped secȝ to þam eorle ;
he polde þæs beornes beaȝas gefecȝan,   160
reaf 7 hrinȝas 7 ȝerenod spurd.

Þa Byrhtnoð bræd bill of sceðe
brad 7 bruneccȝ, 7 on þa byrnan sloh.
To raþe hine ȝelette lidmanna sum,
þa he þæs eorles earm amyrde.   165
Feoll þa to foldan fealohilte spurd :
ne mihte he ȝehealdan heardne mece,
pæpnes pealdan. Þa ȝyt þæt pord ȝecpæð

162 Þa *begins p.* 10a, *fol.* 60a : *so E,* Ða *H.*

---

149 *drenȝa sum :* ' one of the (viking) warriors '. It is note-
worthy that the word *drenȝ* (adopted from ON) implies a warrior
of the viking host. This is the very term that Scandinavian runic
inscriptions of the time use of viking warriors. Thus the Hedeby
stone (L. F. A. Wimmer, *De dansbo Runemindesmærker* no. 72)
commemorates one of Swegen's men who fell *þá drængjaa sátu um
Héðabý* ' when the bold warriors laid siege to Hedeby ' (Slesvig).
These *drængjaa* were Swedish vikings, and their attack was one
of the factors that drew Swegen back from England in 994 (see
Introd. p. 12).

156 *forheardne :* alliterates with *f,* while the similarly formed
adj. *formoni* in 239 alliterates with *m.* This variation is permitted
by the variable stress of the prefix : similarly, the noun *forwyrd,*
for example, in the *Christ* alliterates with *w* in 1536 and with *f*
in 1615.

160 *ȝefecȝan* is a late variant of *gefeccan,* the late OE development
of *gefetian.* Other examples of the same consonant combination
spelled *cȝ* are *orcȝeard* and *Muncȝiu,* cited by Sievers, § 196 (3).

har hilderinc, hyssas bylde,
bæd ȝanȝan forð ȝode ȝeferan.   170
Ne mihte þa on fotum lenȝ fæste ȝestandan ;
he to heofenum plat :
' Ic ȝeþancie þe, ðeoda Paldend,
ealra þæra pynna þe ic on porulde ȝebad.
Nu ic ah, milde Metod, mæste þearfe   175
þæt þu minum ȝaste ȝodes ȝeunne,
þæt min sapul to ðe siðian mote
on þin ȝepeald, Þeoden enȝla,
mid friþe ferian. Ic eom frymdi to þe
þæt hi helsceaðan hynan ne moton.'   180

Ða hine heopon hæðene scealcas,
7 beȝen þa beornas þe him biȝ stodon,
Ælfnoð 7 Pulmær beȝen laȝon,
ða onemn hyra frean feorh ȝesealdon.

Hi buȝon þa fram beadupe þe þær beon noldon : 185
þær purdon Oddan bearn ærest on fleame,
Ɉodric fram ȝuþe, 7 þone ȝodan forlet
þe him mæniȝne oft mear ȝesealde.
He ȝehleop þone eoh þe ahte his hlaford,

171 ȝestandan : ȝe stundan E. 173 ic *supplied*; ȝeþancie : ȝe
þance E. 189 his *begins p.* 10b *and fol.* 60b.

169 *har hilderinc :* see Introd. p. 17.
181 *Ða hine heopon : Liber Eliensis* says that the vikings cut
off Byrhtnoð's head in the thick of the fighting, but these words
of the poem seem to mean only that they slew him. They probably
did not decapitate him until the battle was over. Cf above, p. 8.

183 This line has no alliteration and is probably corrupt. Most
editors adopt Grein's emendation of *beȝen* to *bepeȝen*, interpreted
as ' slain '. This would be a different verb from the recorded
bepeȝan ' cover ', and probably the sense ' slay ' can only be ascribed
to *peȝan* when it has the prefix *for-* (see l. 228). Even *forpeȝen*
will not do here, as concord (strictly observed in past participles
in this poem) requires *forpeȝene*, which would make a much more
difficult emendation. Probably the copyist's eye caught *beȝen*
earlier in the sentence, and he wrote this word again, instead of some
word now irrecoverable ; it may not have resembled *beȝen* at all.
forpeȝene as in 228 or *on* (þam) *pæle* as in 279, 300 would provide the
necessary alliteration, and the latter would be preferable metrically.

on þam ʒerædum þe hit riht ne þæs,   190
7 his broðru mid him beʒen ærndon,
Ʒodpine 7 Ʒodpiʒ ʒuþe ne ʒymdon,
ac pendon fram þam piʒe 7 þone pudu sohton,
fluʒon on þæt fæsten 7 hyra feore burʒon,
7 manna ma þonne hit æniʒ mæð þære,   195
ʒyf hi þa ʒeearnunʒa ealle ʒemundon
þe he him to duʒuþe ʒedon hæfde.
Spa him Offa on dæʒ ær asæde
on þam meþelstede, þa he ʒemot hæfde,
þæt þær modelice maneʒa spræcon   200
þe eft æt þearfe þolian noldon.

   Þa pearð afeallen þæs folces ealdor,
Æþelredes eorl. Ealle ʒesapon
heorðʒeneatas þæt hyra heorra læʒ.
Þa ðær pendon forð plance þeʒenas,   205
unearʒe men efston ʒeorne :
hi poldon þa ealle oðer tpeʒa,
lif forlætan oððe leofne ʒeprecan.

   Spa hi bylde forð bearn Ælfrices,
piʒa pintrum ʒeonʒ pordum mælde,   210
Ælfpine þa cpæð, he on ellen spræc :
'Ʒemunaþ þara mæla þe pe oft æt meodo spræcon,

---

191 ærndon : ærdon E.   192 Ʒodpine : ʒodrine E.   201 þearfe :
þære E.   202 þa : so E, Ða H.   208 forlætan : for lætun E.
212 Ʒemunaþ þara : ʒe munu þa E.

---

190 þe hit riht ne þæs : þe is probably the relative, and the construction is elliptical : ' on those trappings which it was not right
(to mount on) '. The usc of hit as impersonal subject where earlier
syntax would have no pronoun is found also in 66 and 195. It is
perhaps not impossible to take þe as the conj. (BT, s.v. sense III),
but the construction is less natural.

192 ʒymdon : the ʒ of this word being palatal does not enter
into the alliterative scheme of the line, which is therefore normal :
see note to 32.

193 þone pudu : probably the same as the holt in l. 8.

194 fæsten : not a fortress, but a place of safety, the pudu of
the preceding line.

þonne þe on bence beot ahofon,
hæleð on healle ymbe heard ȝepinn :
nu mæȝ cunnian hpa cene sy.   215
Ic pylle mine æþelo eallum ȝecyþan,
þæt ic þæs on Myrcon miccles cynnes ;
þæs min ealda fæder Ealhelm haten,
þis ealdorman þoruldȝesæliȝ.
Ne sceolon me on þære þeode þeȝenas ætþitan   220
þæt ic of ðisse fyrde feran pille,
eard ȝesecan, nu min ealdor liȝeð
forheapen æt hilde. Me is þæt hearma mæst :
he þæs æȝðer min mæȝ 7 min hlaford.'
Þa he forð eode, fæhðe ȝemunde,   225
þæt he mid orde anne ȝeræhte
flotan on þam folce, þæt se on foldan læȝ
forpeȝen mid his pæpne. Onȝan þa þinas manian,
frynd 7 ȝeferan, þæt hi forð eodon.
Offa ȝemælde, æscholt asceoc :   230
' Hpæt, þu, Ælfpine, hafast ealle ȝemanode
þeȝenas to þearfe. Nu ure þeoden lið
eorl on eorðan, us is eallum þearf
þæt ure æȝhpylc oþerne bylde
piȝan to piȝe, þa hpile þe he pæpen mæȝe   235
habban 7 healdan, heardne mece,
ȝar 7 ȝod spurd. Us Ꝺodric hæfð,
earh Oddan bearn, ealle bespicene.
Þende þæs formoni man, þa he on meare rad,
on plancan þam picȝe, þæt þære hit ure hlaford.   240
For þan þearð her on felda folc totpæmed,

217 þæt (þ') *begins þ. 11a, fol. 61a.*   224 æȝðer : æȝder *E.*
233 eorðan : eorðā *E.*

218 *ealda fæder :* rightly interpreted by Ker in 1887 as ' grand-
father '. The parallels cited by M. Ashdown leave no doubt that
this is the sense of the word. In ASC (D) 1016 it is said that
Eadmund cynȝ is ȝebyrȝed mid his ealdan fæder Eadȝare, where
Eadmund is the son of Æþelred. So also in OFris *aldefeder* and in
ME *aldeuader* mean ' grandfather '.

scyldburh tobrocen. Abreoðe his anȝin,
þæt he her spa maniȝne man aflymde.'
Leofsunu ȝemælde 7 his linde ahof,
bord to ȝebeorȝe ; he þam beorne oncpæð : 245
' Ic þæt ȝehate, þæt ic heonon nelle
fleon fotes trym, ac pille furðor ȝan,
precan on ȝepinne minne pinedrihten.
Ne þurfon me embe Sturmere stedefæste hælæð
pordum ætpitan, nu min pine ȝecranc, 250
þæt ic hlafordleas ham siðie,
pende fram piȝe ; ac me sceal pæpen niman,
ord 7 iren.' He ful yrre pod,
feaht fæstlice, fleam he forhoȝode.
Dunnere þa cpæð, daroð acpehte, 255
unorne ceorl ofer eall clypode,
bæd þæt beorna ȝehpylc Byrhtnoð prece :
' Ne mæȝ na pandian se þe precan þenceð
frean on folce, ne for feore murnan.'
Þa hi forð eodon, feores hi ne rohton. 260

---

243 spa *begins p.* 11b; *fol. 61b is not recorded, but probably
begins here.* 257 prece : *so E,* præce *H.*

---

242 *abreoðe his anȝin :* ' may his conduct have an evil end ',
i.e. ' curse him for behaving thus '.

256 *unorne ceorl :* ' simple yeoman '. Dunnere is *unorne* compared with the others who exhort the fighters, because they are
men of rank. Some scholars have taken *unorne* to mean ' old ',
and Dunnere would then be a figure similar to Byrhtwold (cf l. 317).
It must be admitted that the passages quoted in BT at first seem
to support that interpretation. The sense ' simple ' is not otherwise in evidence until ME times, and the only OE instance of the
related *unornlic* is in Ælfric's rendering of *vetera vestimenta* as
unornlic scrud (Joshua ix. 4). But the positive form *or(e)ne* means
' excessive ' and has no reference to youth or age (see the passages
cited s.v. in BT Supplement and Clark Hall's *A.S. Dictionary*), and
etymologically the word is probably composed of *or + hiene* ' not
mean '. Hence the earlier sense of *unorne* is probably ' mean ' or
' humble ', passing into ' plain, simple '. *unornlic* in the Ælfric
passage bears a strong contextual colouring ; this becomes evident
when it is seen that in the same passage he renders *saccos veteres*
as *forperede fetelsas.*

Onȝunnon þa hiredmen heardlice feohtan,
ȝrame ȝarberend, 7 ȝod bædon
þæt hi moston ȝeprecan hyra pinedrihten
7 on hyra feondum fyl ȝepyrcan.
Him se ȝysel onȝan ȝeornlice fylstan ;   265
he pæs on Norðhymbron heardes cynnes,
Ecȝlafes bearn ; him pæs Æscferð nama.
He ne pandode na æt þam piȝpleȝan,
ac he fysde forð flan ȝenehe ;
hpilon he on bord sceat, hpilon beorn tæsde,   270
æfre embe stunde he sealde sume wunde,
þa hpile ðe he pæpna pealdan moste.

Þa ȝyt on orde stod Eadpeard se lanȝa
ȝearo 7 ȝeornful ; ȝylppordum spræc
þæt he nolde fleoȝan fotmæl landes,   275
ofer bæc buȝan, þa his betera leȝ.
He bræc þone bordpeall 7 pið þa beornas feaht,
oð þæt he his sincȝyfan on þam sæmannum
purðlice prec, ær he on pæle leȝe.

Spa dyde Æþeric, æþele ȝefera,   280
fus 7 forðȝeorn feaht eornoste,
Sibyrhtes broðor 7 spiðe mæniȝ oþer,

269 fysde *begins p. 12a, fol. 62a.* 273 þa : *so E,* Ða *H.*
274 ȝearo : *so E,* ȝearc *H.* 279 leȝe : *so E,* læȝe *H.*

266 *on Norðhymbron :* it is not known why Byrhtnoð should
have a hostage from Northumbria ; see Introd. p. 17. The part
played by Æscferð in the fight is in accordance with the best Germanic tradition : the noble hostage was usually treated in the
same way as his host's own followers of equal rank, and the hostage
gave like service in return. Cf the behaviour of the Welsh hostage
in the ASC 755 ; and in *Waltharius* Attila's Germanic hostages
Waltharius and Hagano fight for him.

277 *bræc þone bordpeall :* this is taken by some editors to refer
to the English formation : ' he rushed out from the (English)
shield-rank '. But probably *brecan* was too strong a word to be
used of one man leaving the rank. Moreover *brecan* combined in
alliterative phrases with such words as *bordhreoða* elsewhere refers
to the attack (*Elene* 122). Eadweard broke the Danish line and
fought hand to hand with individual Danes.

clufon cellod bord, cene hi peredon.
Bærst bordes læriʒ, 7 seo byrne sanʒ
ʒryreleoða sum. Þa æt ʒuðe sloh   285
Offa þone sælidan þæt he on eorðan feoll,
7 ðær Ȝaddes mæʒ ʒrund ʒesohte :
hraðe pearð æt hilde Offa forheapen.
He hæfde ðeah ʒeforþod þæt he his frean ʒehet,
spa he beotode ǽr pið his beahʒifan,   290

288 hraðe : raðe *E*.

---

283 *cellod bord :* many guesses have been made at the meaning
and etymology of *cellod*, but it remains a pure mystery. *celaes
borð* in *Finnesburh* 31 is commonly believed to be a corruption of
the same phrase *cellod bord*, but the passage brings us no nearer the
meaning. For the various suggestions that have been made see
R. W. Chambers's note on *Finnesburh* 31 in his edition of *Beowulf*,
p. 160, and B. Dickins on the same passage, *Runic and Heroic
Poems*, p. 67.

284 *læriʒ :* this word occurs only here and in *Exodus* 239. According to M. Förster (*Keltisches Wortgut im Englischen*, Festgabe
für Liebermann, 1921) *læriʒ* is probably a borrowing of Latin *lōrīca*
through the intermediary of Old Welsh, though the phonology of
the short *æ* in *læriʒ* is admittedly difficult, in the face of Welsh
llurig. Welsh *llurig* (with *u* from *ō*) has either been reinfluenced
by the classical form, or the OE word is derived from some British
or Gallo-roman form other than the ancestor of the Welsh word.
The form originally adopted must have been *laríg*, with *ō* shortened
before the stress ; cf OE *sioor* from *secūrus*. Förster questions
whether the *læriʒ* can be the metal rim of the shield (as most
editors had explained the word), and he suggests that it was
rather the metal-studded leather covering of the shield. The use
of the related verb, however, supports the interpretation ' border ',
' rim '; the verb occurs in the gloss *syn emblǽrʒide* (v.l. *syn
emblærʒ[ede]*) on *ambiuntur*, where it means ' provide with a
border '—in this instance an ornamental border on the sleeve :
see A. S. Napier, *Old English Glosses* 170/377, and in Anglia **xv.**
207.

288 *hraðe ; raðe* E. *hraðe* and *raðe* were common variants from
an early period : in *Beowulf* both forms were used. Normally in
OE verse *hraðe* in such a line as this was not required to alliterate,
but in this poem the type of half-line found here always has both
lifts alliterating : cf the first half of 8, 227, 232, 248, 274, 302, 312
and the similar 110 and 111.

þæt hi sceoldon beʒen on burh ridan
hale to hame oððe on here crincʒan,
on pælstope pundum speltan.
He læʒ ðeʒenlice ðeodne ʒehende.
Ða pearð borda ʒebræc. Brimmen podon   295
ʒuðe ʒeʒremode. Ʒar oft þurhpod
fæʒes feorhhus. Forð ða eode Pistan,
Ƿurstanes suna pið þas secʒas feaht.
He pæs on ʒeþranʒ hyra þreora bana,
ær him Piʒelmes bearn on þam pæle læʒe.   300
Pær pæs stið ʒemot. Stodon fæste
piʒan on ʒepinne. Piʒend cruncon
pundum periʒe. Pæl feol on eorþan.
Ospold 7 Eadpold ealle hpile,
beʒen þa ʒebroþru beornas trymedon,   305
hyra pinemaʒas pordon bædon

---

292 crincʒan : crintʒan *E*.   294–5 hende ... brimmen *begins fol.* 62b.   295 podon *begins p.* 12b.   297 forð ða : forða *E*. 300 Piʒelmes : piʒelines *E*.

---

291 *burh :* this might be Maldon, which was a *burh* in the technical sense of a fortified place, and it would be a natural base for Byrhtnoð in this campaign ; perhaps it was there he held his *ʒemot* (199). But the reference to riding ' home ' in 292 suggests rather that the *burh* was Byrhtnoð's chief residence. Other instances of *burh* in the sense ' manor-house ' occur in KCD 183 and 870, and in *Rectitudines*, Gerefa 13 (Liebermann i. 454) ; and from Alfred's laws 40 (ibid. i. 72) it appears that the dwelling of any man above the rank of *ceorl* was a *burh*.

297–300 The difficulties of this passage have not been finally cleared up. It is unlikely that *Purstanes sunu* is a different person from *Pistan*, as it is contrary to the normal practice of OE poets to name a man by his patronymic without giving his own name as well. For the same reason *Piʒelmes bearn* must refer to some person in the near context. It is usually assumed that Pigelm is another name for þurstan ; but less difficulty is encountered if we take *Piʒelmes bearn* as a description of Offa. The implication seems to be that after Offa was smitten down Pistan slew three of the enemy before Offa (now probably the leader of the English) was finally despatched, just as the mortally wounded Byrhtnoð was protected for a brief moment by the two who stood by him (171–84).

þæt hi þær æt ðearfe þolian sceoldon,
unpaclice pæpna neotan.

   Byrhtpold maþelode, bord hafenode—
se pæs eald ȝeneat—æsc acpehte;   310
he ful baldlice beornas lærde:
' Hiȝe sceal þe heardra, heorte þe cenre,
mod sceal þe mare, þe ure mæȝen lytlað.
Her lið ure ealdor eall forheapen,
ȝód on ȝreote. A mæȝ ȝnornian   315
se ðe nu fram þis piȝpleȝan pendan þenceð.
Ic eom frod feores. Fram ic ne pille,
ac ic me be healfe minum hlaforde,
be spa leofan men licȝan þence.'
Spa hi Æþelȝares bearn ealle bylde   320

310 *eald ȝeneat : eald* probably means primarily ' of long service ',
' trusty ', though the *eald ȝeneat* might, like Byrhtwold, also grow
old in his long service. It is not unlikely that the whole expression
is really a single term, like *ealdȝesiðas* in *Beowulf* 853. The *ȝeneat*
was ordinarily ' a member of the free peasant class, who had a
holding and paid his lord both food-rent and services. One of his
duties was to ride on his lord's errands ' (F. E. Harmer, *English
Historical Documents*, p. 108, with a reference to *Rectitudines* 2 in
Liebermann I. 445). In poetry the word may mean nothing more
precise than ' liegeman ', ' retainer ', and perhaps has that sense
here ; but if this Byrhtwold is identical with Brihtwold *cniht* (see
below, p. 83), then *ȝeneat* has its usual limited meaning, and Byrhtwold was a close personal retainer to Byrhtnoð, as he had been to
Æðelflæd.

313 *mæȝen* probably refers to the bodily strength, which growo
woaker (*lytlað*) from wounds and exhaustion ; but the word might
refer to the English force which is steadily diminishing. Liebermann
evidently took the latter view when he compared *paucis suorum
superstitibus* in *Liber Eliensis*, said of Byrhtnoð's force when the
Danes made their final attack : see p. 8.

315 *a mæȝ ȝnornian :* not ' may he ever mourn '; the use of
mæȝ in an optative sense is unknown in OE, as Wyatt rightly
observes. The sense is rather : ' he has cause to mourn ever ',
i.e. the man who flees now will spend the rest of his life regretting it.
For this use of *mæȝ* cf *Genesis* 799 : *Nu wit magon sorgian for þis
siðe*, and *Christ* 127. The retainer who fled lordless from battle
was regarded in the same way as in Tacitus' time : *vero infame in
omnem vitam ac probrosum superstitem principi suo ex acie recessisse*

Ʒodric to ȝuþe.   Oft he ȝar forlet,
pælspere pindan on þa picinȝas ;
spa he on þam folce fyrmest eode,
heop 7 hynde, oð þæt he on hilde ȝecranc.
Næs þæt na se Ʒodric þe ða ȝuðe forbeah.   325

324 oð : od E.   325 ȝuðe : ȝude E.

SELECT BIBLIOGRAPHY

I. BIBLIOGRAPHICAL LISTS

1885 R. Wülcker, *Grundriss zur Geschichte der angelsächsischen Litteratur*, 334–8, 515

1898 in F. Liebermann's article in Archiv xci. 15, *passim*

[1904] W. J. Sedgefield, *Maldon*, 45–8

1930 M. Ashdown, *English and Norse Documents, passim*

1931 A. H. Heusinkveld and E. J. Bashe, *A Bibliographical Guide to Old English*, 84

1936 E. D. Laborde, *Byrhtnoth and Maldon*, 162–6.

II. THE LOST MANUSCRIPT

1696 Thomas Smith, *Catalogus Librorum Manuscriptorum Bibliothecae Cottonianae*, 67

1705 H. Wanley, *Librorum Vett. Septentrionalium, qui in Angliæ Bibliothecis extant...Catalogus Historico-Criticus*, 232

1726 Thomas Hearne, *Johannis Confratris et Monachi Glastoniensis Chronica sive Historia de Rebus Glastoniensibus*, I. li and II. 570 f

1904 W. H. Stevenson, *Asser's Life of King Alfred*, xxxii f

III. EDITIONS

Not all the texts printed in readers and primers are listed here.

1726 Thomas Hearne, *Johannis Confratris et Monachi Glastoniensis Chronica sive Historia de Rebus Glastoniensibus*, II. 570 f

1834 B. Thorpe, *Analecta Anglo-Saxonica*, 131–41 (Revised ed. 1846)

1835 Ludv. Chr Müller, *Collectanea Anglo-Saxonica maximam partem nunc primum edita et vocabulario illustrata*, 52–62

1847 F. W. Ebeling, *Angelsächsisches Lesebuch*, 85–93

1849 L. Klipstein, *Analecta Anglo-Saxonica*, II. 261–79

1850 L. Ettmüller, *Engla and Seaxna Scopas and Boceras*, 133–40

1857 Chr. W. M. Grein, *Bibliothek der angelsächsischen Poesie*, I. 343–52

1861 M. Rieger, *Alt- und angelsächsisches Lesebuch*, 84–94

1876 H. Sweet, *Anglo-Saxon Reader*, 133–44 (4th ed. with revised text 1884 ; 9th ed. revised C. T. Onions 1922)

1880 K. Körner, *Einleitung in das Studium des Angelsächsischen*, 2. teil : texte, 72–88

THE BATTLE OF MALDON

1881   J. Zupitza, *Alt- und mittelenglisches Übungsbuch* (5th ed. Schipper; 12th ed. Eichler 1921)

1883   R. Wülcker, *Bibliothek der angelsächsischen Poesie*, I. 358–73 (Revision of Grein above under 1857)

1888   F. Kluge, *Angelsächsisches Lesebuch*, 120–7 (4th ed. 1915)

1897   C. L. Crow, *Maldon and Brunanburh*

[1904]   W. J. Sedgefield, *The Battle of Maldon and short poems from the Saxon Chronicle*

1919   A. J. Wyatt, *Anglo-Saxon Reader*, 188–97

1922   W. J. Sedgefield, *An Anglo-Saxon Verse Book* (reprinted 1928 in *An Anglo-Saxon Book of Verse and Prose*)

1930   M. Ashdown, *English and Norse Documents relating to the reign of Ethelred the Unready*

1936   E. D. Laborde, *Byrhtnoth and Maldon*

IV. TRANSLATIONS

1826   J. J. Conybeare, *Illustrations of Anglo-Saxon Poetry*, xc f

1887   H. W. Lumsden, in *Macmillan's Magazine* iv. 371 f. Reprinted in A. S. Cook and C. B. Tinker, *Select Translations from Old English Poetry* 1902 (revised ed. 1926)

1887   (but published in 1926) W. P. Ker in R. W. Chambers, *England before the Norman Conquest*, 260 f.

1930   M. Ashdown (as above)

V. TEXTUAL AND LITERARY STUDIES AND NOTES

1882   U. Zernial, *Das Lied von Byrhtnoð's Fall*, 991

1894   D. Abegg, *Zur Entwicklung der historischen Dichtung bei den Angelsachsen*

1908   W. P. Ker, *Epic and Romance*, 54–7

1919   O. F. Emerson in MLR xiv. 205–7

1921   F. Klaeber, *Zu Byrhtnoðs Tod*, Englische Studien lv. 390

1924   E. D. Laborde, *The Style of the Battle of Maldon*, MLR xix. 401–17

1927   C. Brett, MLR xxii. 260 (on line 48)

1929   B. S. Phillpotts, *The Battle of Maldon : some Danish Affinities*, MLR xxiv. 172–90

1929   F. Klaeber, *Jottings on Old English Poems*, Anglia liii. 227 f

VI. HISTORICAL STUDIES

1867   E. A. Freeman, *The Norman Conquest*; 2nd ed. I. 268 f

1882   J. C. H. R. Steenstrup, *Normannerne* III. 228 f

1895   Notes to Crawford Ch

1898   F. Liebermann, *Zur Geschichte Byrhtnoðs des Helden von Maldon*, Archiv ci. 15 f

1925   E. D. Laborde, *The Site of the Battle of Maldon*, English Historical Review xl. 161 f

1937   E. V. Gordon, *Olaf and Maldon*, MLR xxxii. 24.

SELECT BIBLIOGRAPHY

VII. HISTORICAL SOURCES

1839-48 *Codex Diplomaticus Ævi Saxonici*, ed. J. M. Kemble. (Includes various charters relating to Byrhtnoð and his kin)

1848 *Liber Eliensis*, ed. D. J. Stewart, especially II. 62 f

1848 *Florentii Wigornensis Chronicon* in *Monumenta Historica Britannica*, ed. Petrie and Hardy, vol. II. 580

1861 *The Anglo-Saxon Chronicle*, ed. B. Thorpe (Rolls Series), 238-40. (See also C. Plummer, *Two Saxon Chronicles Parallel*, 1892-99, I. 126-7 and II. 173 f)

1886 *Chronicon Abbatiæ Rameseiensis*, ed. W. D. Macray (Rolls Series), 116-7.

1886 *Vita Oswaldi* in *Historians of the Church of York and its Archbishops*, ed. J. Raine, Rolls Series. Accounts of Byrhtnoð, vol. I. 445 and 455 f (at Maldon)

1882 *Symeonis Monachi Historia Ecclesiæ Dunhelmensis*, ed. T. Arnold, Rolls Series. (Notice of battle of Maldon anno dccccxci, II. 134)

1885-93 *Cartularium Saxonicum*, ed. W. de Gray Birch. (Various charters relating to Byrhtnoð and his kin in vol. III.)

1895 *The Crawford Collection of Early Charters and Documents*, ed. A. S. Napier and W. H. Stevenson. (Byrhtnoð appears in charter 5, and charter 9 is the will of Leofwine, son of the Wulfstan who guarded the bridge at Maldon)

1898 f *Die Gesetze der Angelsachsen*, ed. F. Liebermann. (Text of treaty between Æðelred and the vikings, naming leaders who fought at Maldon, I. 220 f. Also in A. J. Robertson, *Laws of the Kings of England from Edmund to Henry I*, 56 f)

1930 *Anglo-Saxon Wills*, ed. D. Whitelock. (Wills of Byrhtnoð's wife, sister-in-law, and other relatives)

THE SCANDINAVIAN SOURCES

1825-37 *Fornmanna sögur*, 12 vols. containing in vol. I–III *Óláfs saga Tryggvasonar* (the longest and latest form of the saga ; transl. by J. Sephton, 1895). In vol. X another version of the saga, more closely based on the lost Latin history of Oddr Snorrason ; this version also ed. Finnur Jónsson, *Saga Óláfs Tryggvasonar*, Copenhagen, 1932

1893-1900 *Heimskringla*, ed. Finnur Jónsson. Contains Snorri Sturluson's version of *Óláfs saga* ; for Olaf in the British Isles see I. 292 f. (Trans. S. Laing 1844, reprinted Everyman's Library 1915-30 ; W. Morris and Magnusson, Saga Library, 1893-1905 ; E. Monsen and A. H. Smith 1931)

See also pp. 13, 14 and notes.

GLOSSARY

In the Glossary words will be found under the forms in which they occur, except that nouns, pronouns and adjectives (excluding irregular comparatives and the like) will be found under the nominative singular (masculine), and the verbs normally under the infinitive. Pronouns occurring only as plural forms will be found under the nominative plural. Some incomplete verbs are entered under the present or past forms that occur in the poem, namely *dēah, mōst, nelle, sceal,* and the past tense *ēode*; and the different stems of the verb ' to be ' also are entered separately. Irregular grammatical or phonological forms likely to offer difficulty will be found in their own alphabetical place with a cross-reference to the entries where they are treated.

The order of letters is alphabetical. *æ* is found as a separate letter after *a*; *þ, ð* are placed after *t*, and their use is normalized, so that *þ* is employed at the beginning of a word or element of a compound, but *ð* in other positions. *ǫ* and the special Old English characters *ȝ* and *ƿ* are replaced by *æ*, g and w respectively.

For other commonly accepted abbreviations see the earlier volumes published in this series.

A

ā, *adv.* always, ever, 315

ābēodan, *v.(2),* announce, deliver (a message) ; **ābēod,** *imper.sg.* 49 (absol. use) ; **ābēad,** *p.t.* 27

ābrēoðan, *v.(2),* fail, 242

ac, *conj.* but 82, 193, 247, 252, 269, 318

ācweccan, *w.v.(1c),* shake, brandish ; **ācwehte,** *p.t.* 255, 310

āfeallan, *v.(7),* fall, be laid low (in death), 202 (*p.pt.*)

āflȳman, *w.v.(1b),* put to flight, cause to flee, 243

āfȳsan, *w.v.(1b),* drive away 3n

āgan, *pret.-pres.v.* own, have ; **āh,** *pres.1sg.* 175 ; **āhte,** *p.t.* 189 ; *upgang agan,* be allowed passage 87

āgyfan, *v.(5),* give, render ; **āgeaf,** *p.t.* 44 ; **āgyfen,** *p.pt.* 116

āh, see **āgan**

āhebban, *v.(6),* raise ; utter loudly ; **āhōf,** *p.t.* raised 130, 244 ; **āhōfon,** *p.t.pl.* uttered loudly 213 ; **āhafen,** *p.pt.* 106

āhte, see **āgan**

ālȳfan, *w.v.(1b),* allow 90

āmyrran, *w.v.(1b),* wound, cripple, 165

66

ān, *adj.* one 117, 226
āna, *adv.* alone 94
and, *conj.* and 3, 8, &c.; always abbreviated as 7 in E
andswaru, *f.* answer 44
angin, *n.* beginning; action, behaviour, 242n
anrǣd, *adj.* resolute 44, **132**
ār, *m.* messenger 26
āsǣde, see **āsecgan**
āsceacan, *v.*(6), shake; **āsceōc**, *p.t.* 230
āsecgan, *w.v.*(3), say; **āsǣde**, *p.t.* 198

Æ

ǣfre, *adv.* ever; *æ. embe stunde*, ever and anon, repeatedly, 271
æfter, *prep.w.dat.* after 65
ǣghwylc, *pron.* each; *æ. operne*, one another 234
ǣgðer, *pron.* each (of two), either, 133; *conj.* **ǣgðer** . . . **and**, both . . . and 224*
ǣnig, *pron.* any 70; *adj.* 195
ǣr, *adv.* first, before, 60; (giving pluperf. value to p.t.) 158, 198, 290; *conj.w.subj.* before 279, 300; *correl.w.* **ǣr**, *adv.*, 61
ǣrænde, *n.ja-stem,* message 28
ǣrnan, *w.v.*(1b), gallop 191*
ǣrost, *adv.superl.* first 124; **ǣrest** 186; *þā* . . . *ǣrest,* as soon as 5n
ǣs, *n.* food, carrion, 107
æsc, *m.* spear (of ash wood) 43, 310
æschere, *m.ja stem,* viking army 69n
æscholt, *n.* spear (of ash wood) 230
æt, *prep.w.dat.* at, in, by, 10, 81, 201, 268; followed by noun without def.art. in phrases, as *æt fotum,* 119; *æt hilde,* 48, 55, **123**, 223, 288; so also 104,

145, 201, 212, 285, 307; *æt us,* from us, 39
ætforan, *prep.w.dat.* before, in front of, 16
ætterne, **ættryne**, *adj.* poisoned; deadly, 47, 146n
ætwītan, *v.*(1) *w. dat.,* reproach 220, 250
æðele, *adj.* noble 151, 280
æðelo, *n.ja-stem pl.,* descent, (noble) origin, 216

B

baldlīce, *adv.* boldly 311; **baldlicost**, *superl.* 78
bana, *w.m.* slayer 299
bæc, *n.* back; *ofer bæc,* back 276
bæd, **bǣdon**, see **biddan**
bǣron, **bǣrst**, see **beran**, **berstan**
be, *prep.w.dat.* by, near, 319; *be healfe,* by the side (of) 152, 318; *be þam,* by this 9; **big**, *postpositive stressed form (really adv.)* 182
beadu, *m.wa-stem,* battle; **beaduwe**, *dat.sg.* 185
beadurǣs, *m.* rush of battle, onslaught, 111
bēah, *m.* ring; **bēagas**, *acc.pl.* things of value 31; *precious* trappings 160
bēahgifa, *w.m.* giver of rings, bounteous lord, 290
béarn, *n.* child; son, 92, &c.
becuman, *v.*(4), come; **becōmon**, *p.t.pl.* 58
bēgen, *adj.* both 182, 183, 191, 291, 305
benc, *f.i-stem,* bench 213
bēon, *anom.v.* be, 185; see **eom**, **wæs**
gebeorg, *n.* defence 31, 131, 245
beorgan, *v.*(3)*w.dat.* protect, save; **burgon**, *p.t.pl.* 194

67

béorn, *m.* warrior, fighting-man, soldier, 17, 131, &c.

béot, *n.* vow, 15, 213 ; *on beot,* as a demand, menacingly, 27n

béotian, *w.v.(2),* vow 290

beran, *v.(4),* bear ; *b. gar to guðe,* advance to battle 12 ; *b. garas togædere,* join battle 67 ; *b. bord* (or *linde*), take up shields to advance, advance, 62, 99 ; **bǽron,** *p.t.* 99 ; **béron,** *p.t.subj.* 67

berstan, *v.(3),* burst, be broken ; **bærst,** *p.t.* rang 284

bestándan, *v.(6),* stand around, surround ; **bestódon,** *p.t.pl.* lined (the banks of the Pante) 68

beswícan, *v.(1),* betray ; **beswicene,** *p.pt. acc.pl.* 238

betere, *adj.compar.n.,* better 31 ; *m. as sb.* superior, lord, 276

gebídan, *v.(1) w.gen.,* meet with, experience ; **gebád,** *p.t.* 174

biddan, *v.(5),* ask 87 ; pray 262 ; bid, order, exhort, 20, &c. ; **bæd,** *p.t.* 20, 128, &c. ; **bǽdon,** *p.t.pl.* 87, &c.

big, see **be**

bill, *n.* sword 114, 162

biter, *adj.* grim, fierce, 85, 111

blíðra, *adj.compar.* more joyful, better pleased, 146

blódig, *adj.* bloody 154

boda, *w.m.* messenger 49

boga, *w.m.* bow 110

bórd, *n.* shield 15, &c.

bordweall, *m.* wall of shields 277 ; see 102n

brád, *adj.* broad 15, 163

gebræc, *n.* clash 295

bræd, see **brédan**

brecan, *v(4),* break ; **brocen,** *p.pt.* 1 ; **bræc,** *p.t.* broke through, 277n

brédan, *v.(3),* move quickly ; **bræd,** *p.t.* plucked out 154 ; drew (sword) 162

bréost, *n.pl.* breast 144

bricg, *f.jó-stem,* bridge ; causeway 74, 78

bricgwéard, *m.* guard of the bridge or causeway 85

brimlíðend, *m.nd-stem,* seafarer ; viking 27

brimmen, *m.cons.-stem pl.,* seafarers, vikings, 49, 295

brocen, see **brecan**

bróðor, *m.r-stem,* brother 282 ; *pl.* **bróðru** 191

gebróðru, *m.r-stem pl.* brothers 305

brúneccg, *adj.* bright of blade, with gleaming blade, 163

búgan, *v.(2),* turn (away) ; **bugon,** *p.t.pl.* 185 ; *ofer bæc bugan,* retreat, give way, 276

burgon, see **beorgan**

burh, *f.cons.-stem,* fortified place ; nobleman's manor, 291n

búrþén, *m.* chamberlain 121

búton, *conj.w.subj.* except, unless, 71

býldan, *w.v.(1b),* encourage, embolden, 169, 234, 320 ; *bylde forð,* exhorted to advance 209

byre, *m.i-stem,* opportunity 121

býrne, *w.f.* corslet, coat of mail, 144, 163, 284

bysig, *adj.* busy, at work, 110

C

cáf, *adj.* brisk, valiant, 76

cáflíce, *adv.* boldly, valiantly, 153

cáld, *adj.* cold 91n

gecamp, *m.* battle, 153

ceallian, *w.v.(2),* shout 91n

cellod, *adj.* See 283n

cempa, *w.m.* warrior 119

cēne, *adj.* keen, valiant, 215, 283, 312 (*compar.*)

céorl, *m.* freeman of lowest rank, yeoman, 132, 256

gecēosan, *v.*(2), choose; *wæl-ræste geceas*, met death on the battle-field 113

clēofan, *v.*(2), split, cleave; clufon, *p.t.pl.* 283

clypian, *w.v.*(2), call out 25, 256

cniht, *m.* youth 9, 153

crincgan, *v.*(3), fall, perish, 292*; cruncon, *p.t.pl.* 302

gecríngan, *v.*(3), fall, perish; gecranc, *p.t.* 250, 324

cuman, *v.*(4), come; cōm, *p.t.* 65; cumen, *p.pt.* at hand 104

cunnian, *w.v.*(2), prove, test, 215

cweðan, *v.*(5), say; cwæð, *p.t.* 211, 255

gecweðan, *v.*(5), speak, utter; gecwæð, *p.t.* 168

cynn, *n.ja-stem*, family, kindred, 76, 217, 266

cyrm, *m.* cry, uproar, 107

gecȳðan, *w.v.*(1b), make known, declare, 216

D

daroð, *m.* spear, dart, 149, 255

dæg, *m.* day; *on dæg*, upon a (certain) day 198

dægweorc, *n.* day's work 148

dǽlan, *w.v.*(1b), share; *hilde dælon*, should join battle, 33 (*subj. pl.*). Cf *Beowulf* 2534

dēah, *pres.3 sg.w.dat.* avails, profits, 48

derian, *w.v.*(1a) *w.dat.*, harm 70

dōm, *m.* judgment; stipulation, choice, 38; glory 129

dōn, *anom.v.* do; dyde, *p.t.* did, 280; gedōn, *p.pt.* 197

dreng, *m.* warrior, 149n

Drihten, *m.* Lord, God, 148

duguð, *f.* benefit, help, 197

dyde, see dōn

E

ēac, *prep.w.dat.* in addition to 11

éald, *adj.* old, 47n, 310n; éalda fæder, grandfather 218n

éaldor, *m.* chief, lord, 11, &c.

ealdorman, *m. cons.stem*, nobleman, earl, 219

eall, *adj.* all 304; *pl.* 174, &c.; *hi ealle*, all of them, they all, 63, &c.; *us eallum, us ealle*, 233, 238; *as pron.*, all men 216; *ofer eall*, to all parts (so all could hear), 256; *adv.* all 314

éard, *m.* homeland, country, 53, 58, 222

earh, *adj.* cowardly 238

earm, *m.* arm 165

éarn, *m.* eagle 107

geéarnung, *f.* act deserving gratitude, favour, 196

eart, see eom

ēasteð, *n.* river-bank 63

ebba, *w.m.* ebb-tide 65

ecg, *f.jō-stem*, edge, blade, 60

efstan, *w.v.*(1b), hasten 206 (*p.t.pl.*)

eft, *adv.* again, afterwards, 201; *eft ongean*, in reply, back again, 49, 156

ellen, *n.* courage; *on ellen*, valiantly 211

embe, *prep.w.acc.* round about 249; *æfre embe stunde*, 271, see **æfre; ymbe**, about, concerning, 214

éngel, *m.* angel 178

ēode, *p.t.* went; *fyrmest eode*, went out in the forefront of battle 323; *forð eode* (or pl. *eodon*), advanced, pressed to the front of battle, 225, 229 (*subj.*), 260, 297; *eode to*, approached, 132, 159 eoh, *m.* steed, charger, 189

eom, *pres.1 sg.* am, 179, 317; eart, *2 sg.* art, are, 36; is, *3 sg.* is, 31, 233; sӯ, *subj.sg.* 215. See bēon, wæs

éorl, *m.* earl 6n, 28, 51n, &c.

éornoste, *adv.* resolutely 281

éorðe, *w.f.* earth 107, &c.

ēow, see gē

ēðel, *m.* homeland, one's own country, 52

F

faran, *v.(6),* go, pass, 88; speed 156

fæder, *m.r-stem,* father; *ealda fæder,* grandfather 218n

fǽge, *adj.* doomed, fated, 105, &c.; *as sb.,* 297

fǽgere, *adv.* suitably, well, 22

fæhð(o), *f.* hostility, battle, 225

fǽrsceaða, *w.m.* sudden raider, ravager, viking, 142

fæste, *adv.* firmly, steadily, 21, 103, 171, 301

fæsten, *n.ja-stem,* fastness, place of safety, 194n

fæstlíce, *adv.* stoutly, resolutely, 82, 254

fæstnian, *w.v.(2),* confirm 35

feaht, see feohtan

feallan, *v.(7),* fall 166; fall in battle 54, 105, 111; fall wounded (or dead) 119, 126, 286, 303; fēol(l), *p.t.* 119, 126, &c.; fēollon, *p.t.pl.* 111

fealohilte, *adj.* having a yellow (golden) hilt 166

gefecgan, *w.v.(3),* bear off, take, 160n

fela, *n.indecl.w.gen.* much, many, 73, 90

féld, *m.u-stem,* field of battle 241

fēng, see fōn

feoh, *n.* property; money 39

gefeoht, *n.* fight, 12

feohtan, *v.(3),* fight 16, 261; feaht, *pa.t.* 254, &c.

gefeohtan, *v.(3),* win in battle 129

feohte, *w.f.* battle 103*

fēolheard, *adj.* hard as a file 108n

fēol(l), fēollon, see feallan

fēond, *m.nd-stem,* enemy 103, 264; fӯnd, *acc.pl.* 82

feor, *adv.* far, afar, 3, 57

feorh, *m. or n.* life, 125, &c. fēores, *gen.* 260, 317; fēore, *dat.* 194, 259

feorhhūs, *n.* 'house of life', body, 297

gefēra, *w.m.* comrade, member of the earl's household, 229, 280; *gangan forð gode geferan,* advance stoutly together, 170

fēran, *w.v.(1b),* go, depart, 41, 221

ferian, *w.v.(1a),* go, depart, 179

fēða, *w.m.* troop, force, 88

findan, *v.(3),* find, encounter; fúndon, *p.t.pl.* 85

flān, *m.* arrow, dart, 71, 269

flēam, *m.* flight 81, &c.

flēogan, *v.(2),* fly 7, 109, 150; flee 275

flēon, *v.(2),* flee 247; flugon, *p.t.pl.* 194

flōd, *n.* flood-tide, tide, 65, 72

flot, *n.* deep water, sea, 41

flota, *w.m.* seaman; viking 72, 227

flōwan, *v.(7),* flow 65

flugon, see flēon

flyht, *m.* flight 71

folc, *n.* people, 45, 54, 202; army, host, 22, 227, 241, 259, 323

fólde, *w.f.* earth, ground, 54, 166, 227

folme, *w.f.* hand, 21, &c.

fōn, *v.(7),* seize ; *to wæpnum feng,* took up arms 10

for, *prep.w.dat. for* 96, 259 ; because of 64, 89 ; *for þan* from that cause 241

forbūgan, *v.(2),* flee away from ; **forbēah,** *p.t.* 325

fórd, *m.u-stem,* ford, 81, 88

forgyfan, *v.(5),* give ; **forgeaf,** *p.t.* 139, 148

forgýldan, *v.(3),* buy off, 32

forhéard, *adj.* exceedingly hard 156n

forhēawan, *v.(7),* hew down ; **forhēawen,** *p.pt.* 115, &c.

forhicgan, *w.v.(3),* despise, scorn ; **forhogode,** *p.t.* 254

forhtian, *w.v.(2),* fear, be afraid, 21 *(p.t.subj.)*

forlǣtan, *v.(7),* leave, abandon, 2, 187, 208* ; cause (to go), *w.infin.* as in *forlet faran,* sent speeding forth 156, and so 149, 321 ; **forlēt,** *p.t.* 149, &c.

forma, *adj.superl.* foremost, first, 77

formoni, *adj.* very many, 239

forð, *adv.* forth, onward, 3, **12,** &c. ; *to forð,* too successfully, too deeply, 150

forðgéorn, *adj.* eager to advance 281

geforðian, *w.v.(2),* carry out, accomplish, 289

forwegan, *v.(5),* destroy, kill ; **forwegen,** *p.pt.* 228

fōt, *m.cons.-stem,* foot 119, &c.

fōtmǣl, *n.* foot's length, foot, 275

fram, *prep.w.dat.* away from, 185, &c. ; *adv.* away 317

franca, *w.m.* spear 77n, 140

frēa, *w.m.* lord, 12, &c.

frēod, *f.* peace 39

frēond, *m.nd-stem,* friend ; **frýnd,** *acc.pl.* 229

frið, *m.* peace, 39, 179 ; *gen.* at peace 41

frōd, *adj.* wise, experienced, 140 ; old ; *frod feores,* advanced in years 317

frymdi, *adj.* making request, desirous ; *ic eom frymdi to þe,* I beseech thee 179

ful(l), *adv.* very, right, 153, 253, 311

fúndon, see **fíndan**

furðor, *adv.compar.* further ; *f. gan,* advance 247

fūs, *adj.* eager (to press on) 281

fyl, *m.* death 71, 264

fylstan, *w.v.(1b)w.dat.,* help 265

fȳnd, see **fēond**

fýrd, *f.i-stem,* defensive army, local levy, 221

fyrdrinc, *m.* warrior 140

fyrmest, *adj.superl.* foremost 323. See **ēode**

fȳsan, *w.v.(1b),* send forth rapidly, shoot, 269

G

gafol, *n.* tribute 32, 46 ; **gofol,** 61n

gān, *anom.v.,* go 247 ; **gāð,** *imper.pl.* come, 93. See **ēode**

gángan, *v.(7),* go ; move together, advance, 62 ; *g. forð,* advance 3, 170 ; *to scype gangon (subj.),* should get away to the ships 56 ; *(reflex.) us gangan,* betake ourselves, go (away), 40

gegángan, *v.(7),* win, carry off, 59

gār, *m.* spear 13, &c.

gārberend, *m.nd-stem pl.,* warriors armed with spears 262

gārrǣs, *m.* conflict of spears, battle, 32

gāst, *m.* soul, spirit, 176

gē, *pron.pl.* you, 32, &c. ; **ēow**, *acc.* 41 ; *dat.* 31, 46, 48, 93

gealgean, *w.v.*(2), defend 52n

gearo, *adj.* ready 274 ; **gearowe**, *nom.pl.m.* 72, 100

geóng, *adj.* young 210 ; *wk.*, 155

géorn, *adj.w.gen.* eager (for) 73, 107

géorne, *adv.* eagerly 123, 206 ; readily, clearly, 84

geornful, *adj.* eager 274

geornlīce, *adv.* eagerly, willingly, 265

gif, gyf, *conj.* if 34, 36, 196

gnórnian, *w.v.*(2), mourn, feel sorrow, 315

God, *m.* God 94, 262

gōd, *adj.* good, trusty, 170, 237 ; brave, steadfast, 4, 13 ; noble 315, 187 (*wk.*)

gōd, *n.* that which is good, bliss, 176

gofol, see **gafol**

góld, *n.* gold 35

gram, *adj.* fierce 262 ; *as sb.* foe, enemy, 100

gegremian, *w.v.*(1a), enrage 138, 296

grēot, *n.* sand, dust, 315

grim, *adj.* fierce 61

grimme, *adv.* murderously, cruelly, 109*n

grið, *n.* truce, peace, 35n

grúnd, *m.* ground, land, 287

gegrúnden, *p.pt. of* **gríndan** *or* **gegríndan**, *v.*(3), ground, sharpened, 109

gryrelēoð, *n.* terrible song 285

guma, *w.m.* man 94

gūð, *f.* battle 13, 325* , &c.

gūðplega, *w.m.* ' battle-play ', conflict of battle, 61

gūðrinc, *m.* warrior 138

gyf, see **gif**

gylpword, *n.* vaunting word 274

gȳman, *w.v.*(1)*w.gen.*, heed, care for, 192

gȳsel, *m.* hostage 265

gyst, *m.* stranger 86

gȳt, *adv.* yet ; *þa gyt*, still 168, 273

H

habban, *w.v.*(3), have 236 ; **hafast**, *2pres.sg.* 231 ; **hæfð**, *3sg.* 237 ; **hæfde**, *p.t.* had 13, 121 ; held, 199 ; (*as auxiliary*) 22, 197, &c.

hafenian, *w.v.*(2), raise aloft 42n, 309

hafoc, *m.* hawk, falcon, 8

hāl, *adj.* unhurt, safe and sound, 292

hals, *m.* neck 141

hām, *m.* home 292 ; *acc.* homewards 251

hánd, *f.u-stem*, hand 7, &c. ; *pl.* deeds of arms 4 ; *on gehwæðere hand*, on either side 112 ; **hánda**, *dat.sg.* 149

hār, *adj.* grey-haired, hoary, 169

hātan, *v.*(7), command, order ; **hēt**, *p.t.* 2, &c. ; **hēton**, *pa.t.pl.* 30 ; **hāten**, *p.pt.* named, 75, 218

gehātan, *v.*(7), vow, avow, 246, 289

hæleð, hælæð, *m.cons.-stem pl.*, warriors, heroes, 74, 214, 249

hǣðen, *adj.* heathen, 181 ; *as sb.* 55

hē, *pron.m.* he, 7, &c. ; **his**, *gen.* 11, &c. ; **him**, *dat.* of indirect object, 44, 120, 139, &c. ; *with preps.* 11, 182, 191 ; of reference or possession, 7, 119, 145, 152, 197, 267 ; *refl.* (see **licgan**), 300 ; **hine**, *acc.* 164, 181. See **hēo, hī, hit**

héaldan, *v.*(7), hold, grasp, 14, 20, 236; maintain, keep, guard, 19, 74; *eow friðes healdan,* keep peace with you 41; intr., *h. fæste,* hold fast, stand firm, 102; **héoldon,** *p.t.subj. pl.* 20

gehéaldan, *v.*(7), hold, grip, 167

healf, *f.* side; *him be healfe,* by his side 152, and similarly in 318

heall, *f.* hall 214

héanlic, *adj.* humiliating, shameful, 55

héard, *adj.* hard 167, 236; bitter, dire; 33n, 214; resolute, 312 (*compar.*); brave, hard-fighting, 266; *wiges heard,* fierce in battle 130

heardlíce, *adv.* fiercely 261

hearm, *m.* grief, sorrow 223

héawan, *v.*(7), hew, cut down, slay; **héow,** *p.t.* 324; **héowon,** *p.t.pl.* 181

helsceaða, *w.m.* fiend of hell 180

gehénde, *adj.w.dat.* near 294

héo, *pron.f.* she; **hí,** *acc.* (ref. to the soul), 180

heofonas, *m.pl.* heaven 172

hconon, *adv.* from here 246

hcorra, *w.m.* lord 204

héorte, *w.f.* heart 145; courage 312

heorðgenéatas, *m.pl.* ' sharers of the hearth ', members of a chief's *comitatus,* his closest followers, 204

heorðwerod, *n.* the body of household retainers 24

héow, héowon, see **héawan**

hér, *adv.* here, 36, &c.

here, *m.ja-stem,* fighting host; battle 292

heregeatu, *f.* war-gear 48n

hét, héton, see **hátan**

hí, *pron.pl.* they 19, 46, 307, &c.; *acc.refl.* themselves 82, 283; **hyra,** *gen.* their 20, 38, 306, &c.; of them 70, 133, 299; him, *dat.* (to) them 66, 265. See **hé, héo, hit, sylf**

hicgan, *w.v.*(3), give thought to, be intent on, 4n, 123, 133; intend, purpose, 128; **hogode,** *p.t.* 133, 128 (*subj.*); **hogodon,** *p.t.pl.* 123

hider, *adv.* to this place, hither, 57

hige, *m.i-stem,* thought; courage, temper, 4, 312

hild, *f. jō-stem,* battle 8, 33*, &c.

hilderinc, *m.* warrior 169

híredmen, *m.cons.-stem pl.* household retainers 261

hit, *pron.n.* it 66, &c. See **hé, héo, hí**

hláford, *m.* lord 135, &c.

hláfordléas, *adj.* without lord, lordless, 251

gehléapan, *v.*(7), leap upon, mount; **gehléop,** *p.t.* 189

hléo, *n.wa-stem,* shelter; protector 74

hlihhan, *v.*(6), laugh; **hlóh,** *p.t.* 147

gehlystan, *w.v.*(1), listen, hearken, 92 (*p.t.pl.*)

hogode, hogodon, see hicgan

hóld, *adj.* devoted, attached, 24

holt, *n.* wood, copse, 8n

hors, *n.* horse 2

hraðe, *adv.* quickly, soon, 288*n

hréam, *m.* outcry, clamour, 106

hremm, *m.* raven 106

hring, *m.* ring 161

hringlocan, *w.m.pl.* linked rings of corselet 145

hú, *conj.* how 19

hwá, *interrog.pron.m.* who 95, 124, 215; *indef.pron.* any one, someone, 71; **hwæne,** *accus.* each one 2; **hwæt,** *n.* what 45 hwænne, *conj.w.subj.* until the time when 67

hwæt, *interj.* ho ! 231

gehwæðer, *adj.* either, both, 112

hwīl, *f.* time, while ; *ealle hwile* (*acc.*), all the time 304 ; (*dat. pl.*) *hwilon . . . hwilon*, at one time . . . at another time 270 ; *þā hwīle þe* (*as conj.*), as long as 14, &c.

gehwylc, *pron.* each 128, 257

hȳnan, *w.v.*(*1b*), harm 180 ; (*absol.*) strike, smite, 324

hyra, see hī

gehȳran, *w.v.*(*1b*), hear, 45, 117

hyse, *m.ja-stem* (*orig.i-stem*), *inflected stem usually* hyss- (Sievers § 263, n. 3), young man, young warrior, 2, 128, 141, 152 ; hyssas, hysas, *nom.pl.* 112, 123, 169

I

ic, *pron.* I, 117, 173*, 216, &c, ; mē, *accus.* 29 ; mē, *dat.* 5.5 220, 223, 249, 318 (*refl.*). See mīn

in, *adv.* in, inside, 58, 157

īren, *n.* iron, iron blade, 253

is, see eom

L

lāgon, see licgan

lagustrēam, *m.* tidal stream (coming up river) 66

lánd, *n.* land, ground, 90 &c.

láng, *adj.* long ; tall, 273 (*wk.*) ; *to lang þuhte*, seemed too long, seemed tedious, 66

lāð, *adj.* hateful, 86* ; lāðere, *dat.sg.f.* 90 ; lāðre, *compar.n.* 50

lǣdan, *w.v.*(*1b*), lead 88

læg, lǣge, lǣgon, see licgan

lǣran, *w.v.*(*1b*), instruct, exhort, 311

lærig, *m.* rim (of shield) 284n

gelǣstan, *w.v.*(*1b*), serve, help, 11 ; accomplish, carry out, 15

lǣtan, *v.*(*7*), let ; cause 140 ; send forth 7, 108 ; lēt, *p.t.* 7, 140 ; lēton, *p.t.pl.* 108

leg, see licgan

léng, *adv.compar.* longer 171

lēoda, *f.pl.* people 23, 37, 50

lēof, *adj.* dear, favourite, 7*, 208, 319 ; *ðær him leofost wæs*, where he was best pleased to be 23

lēt, lēton, see lǣtan

gelettan, *w.v.*(*1a*), hinder, prevent, 164

licgan, *v.*(*5*), lie, lie slain, 319 (*refl.*) ; ligeð,lið,*pres.3 sg.* 222, 232, 314 ; læg, *p.t.* 157, &c. ; leg, 276 ; lāgon, *p.t.pl.* 112, 183 ; lǣge, *p.t.subj.* 279, 300 (*refl.*)

lidmen, *m.cons.-stem pl.* men of the fleet, vikings, 99, 164

līf, *n.* life 208

lihtan, *w.v.*(*1b*), alight, dismount, 23

línd, *f.* linden wood ; shield 99, 244

lið, see licgan

lūcan, *v.*(*2*), unite, join, 66n

lȳsan, *w.v.*(*1b*), redeem, ransome 37

lytegian, *w.v.*(*2*), use guile 86

lȳtlian, *w.v.*(*2*), grow less 313

M

mā, *n.* more (in number) 195

man (inflected mann-), *m.cons.-stem,* man 77, &c. ; men, *dat.sg.* 125, 319 ; men, *nom.pl.* 105, 206

man, *pron.* one 9

manega, manigne, see mænig

74

manian, *w.v.(2)*, exhort 228 ; **gemanode,** *p.pt.acc.pl.*, 231

māre, *adj. compar.* more, greater, 313. See **mǣst**

maðelian, *w.v.(2)*, speak (at length), make a speech, 42, 309

mæg, *3 sg.pres.* is able, can, 215, 258, 315n ; **mæge,** *pres. subj.* 235 ; **mihte,** *p.t.* 9, 14 *(subj.)*, &c. ; *mihte to,* was able to go to 64

mǣg, *m.* kinsman 5, 114, 224, 287

mægen, *n.* strength 313n

mǣl, *n.* speech 212

mǣlan, *w.v.(1b)*, speak 26n, 43, 210

gemǣlan, *w.v.(1b)*, speak 230, 244

mænig, *adj.* many, many a, 188, 282 ; **manigne,** *acc.m.* 243 ; **manega,** *pl.m.* 200

mǣst, *adj.superl.* greatest 175 ; *as sb.w.gen.* 223. See **māre**

mǣð, *f.* fitness ; what is meet or right 195

mē, see **ic**

mēar, *m.* horse, steed, 188 *(acc.)*, 239

mēce, *m.ja stem,* sword 167, 236

meodo, *m.u-stem,* mead 212

Metod, *m.* Lord, God, 147, 175

meðelstede, *m.i-stem,* meeting-place, meeting, 199

miccle, *adv.* much, 50

micel, *adj.* great, large, much ; **miccles,** *n.gen.sg.* 217

mid, *prep.w.dat.,* with, (going) with, 40, 56 ; in company with, 51, 79, 101, 191 ; among, 23, 76n ; *(of means, instrument)* with, by, 14, 21, 114, &c. ; *(of manner)* 68, 179

mihte, see **mæg**

milde, *adj.* merciful, gentle, 175

mīn, *poss.adj.* my 53, &c.

mōd, *n.* spirit, courage, 313

mōdelīce, *adv.* boldly, vauntingly, 200

mōdi, *adj.* brave, great of spirit, 147 ; **mōdige,** *m.nom.pl.* 80

mōst, *2 sg.pres.* must 30n ; **mōte,** *pres.subj.sg.* may, be permitted, 95, 177 ; **mōton,** *subj.pl.* 180 ; **mōste,** *p.t.* might, was able, 272 ; **mōston,** *p.t.indic. and subj.pl.* 83, 87, 263

gemōt, *n.* meeting, council, 199 ; encounter, conflict, 301

gemunan, *pret-pres.v.w.gen.* remember ; **gemunað,** *imper.pl.* 212* ; **gemunde,** *p.t.* was mindful of, was intent upon, 225 ; **gemundon,** *p.t.pl.w.acc.* remembered 196

múrnan, *v.(3)*, mourn ; *m. for*, trouble about, care for, 96, 259 ; **múrnon,** *p.t.pl.* 96

N

nā, *neg.adv. intensifying* **ne,** not 21, &c.

nama, *w.m.* name 267

genāme, see **geniman**

næs, see **wæs**

ne, *neg.adv.* not 21, &c. ; fused with verbal forms, see **nelle, wæs ;** *as conj.* nor 259

genēat, *m.* follower, retainer, 310n

nēh, *adj.* near 103

genehe, *adv.* frequently 269

nelle, *1 sg.pres.* will not 246 ; **nolde,** *p.t.* would not 6, &c. ; **noldon,** *p.t.pl.* 81, &c.

nēotan, *v.(2)w.gen.,* make use of 308

niman, *v.(4)*, take ; carry off despatch, 252 ; receive 39

geniman, v.(4), take, receive ;
genāme, p.t.subj. 71
nolde, noldon, see nelle
nū, adv. now 93, &c. ; conj. now
that, since, 57, 222, 232, 250

O

of, prep.w.dat. from, out of,
away from, 7, 108, 149, 150,
154, 162, 221
ofer, prep.w.acc. over, across, 88,
&c. ; above 256 ; ofer bæc,
back 276
ōfer, m. bank, shore, 28
ofermōd, n. great pride, over-
confidence, 89
ofscēotan, v.(2), slay with dart ;
ofscēat, p.t. 77
ofstlīce, adv. speedily 143
oft, adv. often, on many occasions, 188, &c.
on, prep.(1)w.dat. on, upon, 25,
28, 63, &c. ; at, in, 142, 153,
199, 214, 248, 302, 324 ;
among, 220, 227, 266, 279,
300, 323 ; of hostile action,
(taken) from, 125, 129 ; (inflicted) on 259, 264, 278 ;
ærest on fleame, first to flee,
186 (2)w.acc. to, onto, into, 58,
163, &c. ; among, into the
midst of, 322 ; (of place) in,
on, 292 (cf Beowulf 635), 299 ;
on flot, to sea 41 ; (of time)
on dæg, on a day 198 ; (in
phrases of manner) on beot,
threateningly 27 ; and so 38,
211
oncnāwan, v.(7), understand,
perceive, 9
oncweðan, v.(5)w.dat. answer,
reply to ; oncwæð, p.t. 245
onemn, prep.w.dat. close by 184
onfíndan, v.(3), perceive ; on-
fúnde, p.t. 5

onfōn, v.(7), receive ; onfēng,
p.t. 110
ongēan, adv. back, in reply, 49,
137, 156 ; prep.w.dat. against
100. See eft
onginnan, v.(3), begin ; ongan,
p.t.w.infin. (forming periphras-
tic p.t.) as ongan alyfan, allowed 89, and so in 12n, 17,
89, 91, 228, 265 ; ongunnon,
pl. 86, 261
ongytan, v.(5), perceive, understand ; ongēaton, p.t.pl. 84
ōrd, m. spear-point, spear, 47n,
60, 110, &c. ; forefront of
battle 273 ; battle-line, array,
69 (or best warriors, the
flower ?)
oð, prep.w.acc. in oð þæt, used
as conj. until 278, 324*
ōðer, adj. and pron. other, another, 64, 70, &c. ; oðer twega,
one of two things 207 ; in
reciprocal phrases, ægðer . . .
oðrum, each other 133 ;
æghwylc oðerne, one another
234
oððe, conj. or, or else, 208, 292

P

prass, m. proud array 68

R

rād, see rīdan
ránd, m. metal centre of shield
by which it is held ; shield,
20*n
raðe, adv. quickly, soon, 30, 164
gerǣcan, w.v.(1c), reach ;
gerǣhte, p.t. pierced 158,
226 ; feorh gerǣhte, pierced
fatally 142
rǣdan, w.v.(1b), instruct 18
gerǣdan, w.v.(1b), decide, determine, 36

76

gerǣdu, *n.ja-stem pl.* trappings 190

rēaf, *n.* spoil, booty, 161

reccan, *w.v.(1c)w.gen.,* care about ; **rohton,** *p.t.pl.* 260

gerēnian, *w.v.(2),* adorn, ornament, 161

ricene, *adv.* quickly 93

rīcost, *adj.superl.* noblest, highest, 36

rīdan, *v.(1),* ride 291 ; **rād,** *p.t.* 18, 239

riht, *adj.* right, fitting, 190

rihte, *adv.* rightly, correctly, 20

rinc, *m.* man, warrior, 18

rohton, see **reccan**

gerȳman, *w.v.(1b),* make way ; *ēow is gerymed,* the way is open to you 93

S

sáng, see **síngan**

sāwul, *f.* soul 177

gesāwon, gesǣde, see **gesēon, gesecgan**

sǣde, see **secgan**

sǣlida, *w.m.* seafarer, viking, 45, 286

sǣmen, *m.cons.-stem.pl.* seafarers, vikings, 29, &c.

sǣrinc, *m.* ' sea-warrior ', viking, 134

scēaf, see **scūfan**

sceaft, *m.* shaft (of spear) 136

sceal, *pres.3 sg.* shall, must, 60, 252 ; must be 312, 313 ; **sceole gē,** *2 pl.* shall you 59 ; **sceolon,** *3 pl.* 54, 220 ; **sceolde,** *p.t.* 16, &c. ; *p.t. subj.* 291, 307

scealc, *m.* retainer, warrior, 181

sceatt, *m.* coin ; tax ; *pl.* tribute-money 40, 56

scēotan, *v.(2),* shoot, hurl ; **scēat,** *p.t.* pierced with dart 143, 270

scēð, *f.* sheath 162

scīr, *adj.* bright, shining, 98n

scūfan, *v.(2),* shove, thrust ; **scēaf,** *p.t.* 136

scýld, *m.* shield 98, 136

scyldburh, *f.cons.-stem,* wall of shields 242 (cf. 102n)

scyp, *n.* ship 40, 56

se, *def.art. (or perhaps demon. adj. in 325), m.* the 6, 69, 155, 273, &c. ; **þone,** *acc.* 19, 77, 286, &c. ; **þæs,** *gen.* 131, 141, 160, 165 ; **þām,** *dat.* 28, 81, 245, &c. ; **sēo,** *f.* 104, 144, 284 ; **þā,** *acc.* 14, 48, 74, 83, &c. ; **þǣre,** *gen.* 95 ; **þǣre,** *dat.* 8, 220 ; **þæt,** *n.* 137 ; *acc.* 22, 102, 168, 194 ; **þæs,** *gen.* 8, 148, 202 ; **þām,** *dat.* 10, 35, 193, &c. ; **þā,** *pl.nom.acc.* 72, 82, 96, 196, &c. ; **þǣra, þāra,** *gen.* 174, 212* ; **þām,** *dat.* 40, 190, 278

sē, *pron.m.* he, it, that one, 75, 150, 227, 310 ; *se þe,* he who 258, 316 ; *(as rel.)* who 27, 153 ; **þæt,** *n.* that 76, 223, 325 ; *acc. (anticipating clause following),* 5, 36*, 84, 246 ; *as rel.,* that which, what, 289 ; **þæs,** *gen.* for this, 120 ; *as adv. because of that,* 299 ; **þām,** *dat.* 9 ; **þan,** *instrum.* 241 ; **þe,** *instr.* by that, the, 146 ; **þe . . . þe,** the . . . as, 312–313 ; **þā,** *pl.nom. as rel.* who 81, 184

(ge)sealde,-on, see **(ge)syllan**

sēcan, *w.v.(1c),* seek, flee to ; **sohton,** *p.t.pl.* 193

gesēcan, *w.v.(1c),* seek, make for, 222 ; *grund gesohte,* was laid low 287

secg, *m.ja-stem,* retainer, man, 159, 298

secgan, w.v.(3), say, tell, 30;
sege'ð, 3 sg.pres. 45; sege,
imper. 50; sæde, p.t. 147
gesecgan, w.v.(3), say; þanc
gesæde, rendered thanks 120
geseman, w.v.(1b), reconcile,
decide the terms between, 60
sendan, w.v.(1b), send 29, 30,
134
seo, see se
geseon, v.(5), see, perceive;
gesawon, p.t.pl. 84, 203
sinc, n. treasure 59
sincgyfa, w.m. 'giver of treasure', bounteous lord, 278
singan, v.(5), sing, ring out;
sang, p.t. 284
siðian, w.v.(2), journey, pass,
177, 251
slean, v.(6), smite, strike; sloh,
p.t. 163, 285; sloge, p.t. subj.
117
snell, adj. keen, bold, 29
softe, adv. easily 59
gesohte, see gesecan
sohton, see secan
spedan, w.v.(1b), be prosperous,
be wealthy, 34n
spell, n. message 50
spere, n.i-stem, spear 108;
spear-head 137
spillan, w.v.(1b), destroy; us
spillan, slaughter each other
34
sprecan, v.(5), speak; spræc,
p.t. 211, 274; spræcon, p.t.pl.
200, 212
sprengan, w.v.(1b), trans.
break, shiver, 137n
springan, v.(3), intrans. spring
(away); sprang, p.t. 137
standan, v.(6), stand (in position) 19, 25, &c.; stand fast,
hold one's ground, 273, 301;
(with predicative adj.) stand
(ready), 72, 100, (steadfast)

127; s. æt, stand fixed in 145;
stynt, 3 sg.pres. 51; stod,
p.t. 25, 28, &c.; stodon,
p.t.pl. 63, 301, &c.
gestandan, v.(6), stand up 171*
stang, see stingan
stæð, n. bank, shore, 25
stede, m.i-stem, place, position,
19
stedefæst, stædefæst, adj.
steadfast, unyielding, 127, 249
stemnettan, w.v.(1b), stand
firm 122n
steppan, v.(6), step, go (forth);
stop, p.t. 8, 78, 131
stihtan, w.v.(1b), direct, order;
incite, exhort, 127
stingan, v.(3), stab, pierce;
stang, p.t. 138
stið, adj. hard; stubborn,
severe, 301
stiðhicgende, pres.pt. firm of
purpose, resolute, 122
stiðlice, adv. stoutly, sternly,
25
stod, stop, see standan, steppan
stream, m. stream 68
stund, f. time, short while;
embe stunde, at brief intervals,
almost every moment 271
stynt, see standan
sum, adj. some 271 (f.acc.sg.);
pron.w.gen. one, a certain one,
149, 164, 285
sunu, suna, m.u-stem, son 76,
298
suðerne, adj. southern, of southern make, 134n
swa, adv. thus, in this way, 122,
198, 209; in like manner, 280,
320, 323; (of degree) so, 33, 59,
243, 319; equally, just as,
132; conj. as 290
sweltan, v.(3), die, perish, 293
sweng, m. blow, stroke, 118

swīðe, *adv.* greatly; fiercely, cruelly, 115, 118; very 282

swúrd, *n.* sword 15, &c.

swustersunu, *m.u-stem*, sister's son 115n

sȳ, see eom

sylf, *adj.* self; hyra sylfra, *gen.pl.* their own 38

syllan, *w.v.(1c)*, hand over, pay, 38, 46; syllon, *pres.subj.pl.* 61; séalde, *p.t.* gave, inflicted, 271

gesyllan, *w.v.(1c)*, give up, give; geséalde, *p.t.* yielded up 188; geséaldon, *p.t.pl.* gave, presented, 184

gesyrwed, *adj.* armed, 159

T

tǽcan, *w.v.(1c)*, show, direct; tæhte, *p.t.* 18

tǽsan, *w.v.(1b)*, lacerate, rive, 270

tīd, *f.i-stem*, time 104

tīr, *m.* glory 104

tō, *prep.w.dat.* to, towards, 8, 13, 56, &c.; *(idiomatically with verbs)* hycgan to, 4, 128, byldan to 235, 321, gemanian to 232; for, as, 46, 131, 197, 245; *to ðam*, to such a degree 34

tō, *adv.* too 55, &c.

tōberstan, *v.(3)*, break, burst asunder; tōbærst, *p.t.* 136, 144

tōbrecan, *v.(4)*, break, break through; tōbrocen, *p.pt.* 242

tōgædere, *adv.* together 67

getoht, *n.* battle 104

tōtwǽman, *w.v.(1b)*, divide, break up, 241

trym, *m. or n.* step, space, 247 (cf. *Beowulf* 2525)

trymian, *w.v.(1a)*, array (in definite order) 17, 22; encourage, exhort, 305; getrymmed, *p.pt.* 22

twēgen, *num.m.* two 80; twēga, *n.gen.* of two things 207

Þ

þā, see se

þā, *adv.* then, thereupon, 2, 62, 143, &c.; *(sometimes used to mark the beginning of a new episode or change of subject)* 17, 25, 149, 181, &c.; *(resumptive, referring to point of time mentioned a little earlier)* 91, 202, 295; correl. with þā 'when' 7, 23, 86; *conj.* when 5*, 10, 16, &c.; since 276. See gȳt

þām, þan, see se, sē

þanc, *m.w.gen.* thanks (for) 120, 147

geþanc, *n.* thought; *god geþanc*, dauntless mind 13

geþancian, *w.v.(2)w.dat.(of pers.)* and gen. thank, render thanks to, 173*

þǽr, *adv.* there 17, 64, &c.; *conj.* where 23, 24, 28

þǽra, þǽre, þæs, see se, sē

þæt, *conj.* that 6, 9, 20, 291, &c.; so that 63, 119, 286, &c.; in that, because, 221, 243, 251. Represented by þ̄ in E except in 36, 136, 263

þæt, *art. and pron.*, see se, sē

þe, *indecl.rel.pron.* who 36, 52, 325, &c.; which, that, 48, 148, 190n; 197

þe, *adv.(instr. of þæt) with compars.*, the 146, 312, 313; *conj.* as, *(correl. with þe, adv.)* 313

þēah, *adv.* however 289

þearf, *f.* need, stress, 175, 201*, 233, 307; *to þearfe*, for (our) good, 232

þearle, *adv.* sorely, grievously, 158

þegen, *m.* (noble) retainer, liegeman, 151, 205, 220, 232

þegenlíce, *adv.* loyally, nobly, as befitting a þegen, 294

þencan, *w.v.(1c)w.infin.* think, intend, 258, 316, 319

þéod, *f.* people 90, 173, 220

þéoden,*m.* prince, lord, 120, &c.

þes, *dem.adj.m.* this ; þisne, þysne, *acc.* 32, 52 ; þís, *instr.* 316 ; þisse, *f.dat.sg.* 221 ; þis, *n.* 45 ; þás, *pl.acc.* these 298

þín, *poss.adj.* thy, your, 37, 50, 178

þincan, *w.v.(1c)*, seem 55 ; þúhte, *p.t.* 66

þis, þisne, see þes

þolian, *w.v.(2)*, endure, hold out, 201, 307

geþolian, *w.v.(2)*, endure 6

þone, see se

þonne, *conj.* when, 213 ; than 33*n, 195

geþráng, *n.* throng, press, 299

þréo, *num.* three ; þréora, *gen.* 299

þú, *pron.* thou, you, 30, &c. ; þé, *dat.* 29, &c.

þúhte, see þincan

þurfan, *pret.-pres.v.* need ; þurfe wé, *1 pl.pres.* 34 ; þurfon, *3 pl.pres.* have cause to 249

þurh, *prep.w.acc.* through 71, 141, 145, 151

þurhwadan, *v.(6)*, pierce, pass through ; þurhwód, *p.t.* 296

þus, *adv.* thus 57

U

unbefohten, *adj.* unopposed, without a fight, 57

unearh, *adj.* undaunted, not craven ; unearge, *nom.pl.* 206

unforcúð, *adj.* noble ; dauntless, 51n

unforht, *adj.* undaunted 79

geunnan, *pret.-pres.v.w.gen.*, grant 176

unórne, *adj.* simple, humble, 256n

unwáclíce, *adv.* without weakening 308

unweaxen, *adj.* not fully grown 152

úp, *adv.* up, on high, 130

upgáng, *m.* landing, passage up on land, 87*n

úre, *poss.adj.* our, 56, &c. ; *pron.gen.* of us 234

út, *adv.* out 72

W

wác, *adj.* slender 43

wácian, *w.v.(2)*, prove soft, 10

wadan, *v.(6)*, pass, advance, 140 ; wód, *p.t.* 130, 253 ; wódon, *p.t.pl.* 96, 295

gewadan, *v.(6)*, pass, penetrate ; gewód, *p.t.* 157

Wáldend, *m.nd-stem*, Lord 173

wánd, see windan

wándian, *w.v.(2)*, flinch, draw back, 258, 268

wát, see witan

wæl, *n.* the slain (in battle) 126, 279, 300, 303

wælræst, *f.* resting-place among the slain, death in battle, 113

wælspere, *n.i-stem*, deadly spear 322

wælstów, *f.* field of battle 95, 293

wælwulf, *m.* wolf of slaughter, fierce warrior, 96

wǽpen, *n.* weapon, 10, 83, &c.

wæs, *p.t.* was 23, 107, 217, &c. ; wǽron, *p.t.pl.* were 110 ; wǽre, *p.t.subj.sg.* 195, 240 ; næs, was not 325. See béon, eom

wæter, *n.* water, river, 64, &c.

wē (*recip.*) *pron.* we 33, &c.;
ūs, *acc.* 34, 60, 237; **ūs**, *dat.*
39, &c., 40. See **ūre**

gewéald, *n.* power 178

wéaldan, *v.*(7)*w.gen.*, wield 83,
168, 272; hold, be master of,
95

wearð, see **weorðan**

wegan, *v.*(5), carry, bear;
wēgon, *p.t.pl.* 98

wēnan, *w.v.*(1b), think, believe,
239

wéndan, *w.v.*(1b), turn, go
(away), 193, 252, 316; **w.**
forð, advance 205

weorðan, *v.*(3), become; hap-
pen, be, **295**; **wearð**, *p.t.*
became, was, 113*, 295; as
auxil. with p.pt., was 106, 114,
116*, &c.; **wurdon**, *p.t.pl.*
in **w.** *on fleame*, took to flight
186; **wurde**, *p.t.subj.* would
be 1

werian, *w.v.*(1a), defend; *hi
weredon*, defended themselves
82, 283

wērig, *adj.* exhausted 303

werod, *n.* band, force of men,
51, 64, 97, 102

west, *adv.* west 97*

wicg, *n.ja-stem*, horse, steed, 240

wīcing, *m.* pirate, viking, 26, 73,
97, 116, 139, 322

wīg, *n.* battle 73, 128, &c.;
wigge, *dat.* 10*n

wiga, *w.m.* warrior 75, 79, **126**,
&c.

wīgend, *m.nd-stem*, warrior 302

wīgheard, *adj.* stern in fight 75

wīgplega, *w.m.* ' play of battle ',
fighting, 268, 316

wīhaga, *w.m.* ' battle-hedge ',
shield-rank, 102n

willan, *anom.v.* be willing 35,
40; desire 216; be resolved
46, 52, 317; *pres. as auxil. of*

future, 247; **wille**, *1 sg.pres.*
221, 247, 317; **wylle**, 216;
wile, *3 sg.* 52; **willað**, *pl.* 35,
40, 46; **wille**, *subj.* 37;
wolde, *p.t.* 11, 129, 160;
woldon, *p.t.pl.* 207. See
nelle

wíndan, *v.*(3), fly, speed away,
322; **wánd**, *p.t.* brandished
43; **wúndon**, *p.t.pl.* circled
round 106

wine, *m. orig. i-stem.*, comrade
228; patron 250

winedrihten, *m.* lord and friend,
patron, 248, 263

winemǣg, *m.* beloved kinsman;
winemāgas, *acc. pl.* 306

gewinn, *n.* battle, strife, 214,
248, 302

gewinnan, *v.*(3), overcome, destroy, 125

winter, *m.u-stem*, winter; year
210

wīs, *adj.* wise 219

wīsian, *w.v.*(2), guide 141

witan, *pret.-pres.v.* know; **wāt**,
3 sg.pres. 94; **wiste**, *p.t.*
24

gewītan, *v.*(1), go (away), depart; **gewāt**, *p.t.* went 72;
sped away 150

wið, *prep.w.gen.* towards, to, 8,
131; *w.dat.* to 290; against
103; in return for 31, 35, 39;
w.acc. against, with, 82, 277,
298

wiðerlēan, *n.* requital 116

wlanc, *adj.* proud, splendid, 139,
205, 240

wlītan, *v.*(1), look; **wlāt**, *p.t.*
172

wōd, **wōdon**, see **wadan**

wolde, **woldon**, see **willan**

wórd, *n.* word, speech, 26, 43,
&c.

woruld, *f.* the world 174

GLOSSARY OF PROPER NAMES

Ælfere, one of the three defenders of the *bricg*, 80.

Ælfnoð, a retainer who stood by Byrhtnoð's side in the battle, 183.

Ælfric, father of Ælfwine, 209. As Freeman suggested, it is probable that he is the Ælfric who became ealdorman of Mercia in 983 and was banished in 985 or 986. According to Florence of Worcester and Henry of Huntingdon this Ælfric was son of the previous ealdorman Ælfhere; but Ælfhere's brother, ealdorman Ælfheah of Hampshire, in his will calls Ælfric's son Ælfwine his ' sister's son ' (BCS 1174, Whitelock ix. 22/28). Ælfric was therefore Ælfhere's brother-in-law, having married a daughter of Ealhelm (possibly the Æðelflæd of KCD 1290, Whitelock iii.). It is to be noted that Ælfwine in 218 claims Ealhelm as ancestor to prove his high descent, and does not mention his father Ælfric, who was not *woruldgesælig*. Ælfric seems to have been banished for purely political reasons, though charges of injustice and violence were also made against him (e.g. in KCD 703).

Ælfwine, kinsman of Byrhtnoð, son of Ælfric (q.v.), grandson of **Ealhelm** (q.v.), and thus a scion of one of the greatest families in Mercia, 211, 231. Ælfwine is with Byrhtnoð because his father had been expelled from his patrimony. In his uncle Ælfheah's will, made about 969, he receives a legacy of land at Froxfield, Hants.

Æscferð, son of **Ecglāf,** a Northumbrian of noble family and a hostage in Byrhtnoð's household, 267

Æðelgār, father of **Godric,** 320

Æðelred, King of England 978–1016 (known as Æðelred II or ' the Redeless '), 53, 151, 203

Æðeric, one of Byrhtnoð's retainers, brother of Sībyrht, 280. Possibly identical with the Essex landowner Æðeric who made a will at some time before 995 (KCD 699; Whitelock xvi. (1), 42). This Æðeric was suspected *þæt he wære on þam unræde þæt man sceolde on Eastsexon Swegen underfon* in 994 (KCD 704, Whitelock xvi. (2) 44), so that if he is the Æðeric of the poem, he must have survived the battle.

Byrhtelm, father of Byrhtnoð, 92.

Byrhtnoð, earl or ealdorman of Essex 956–91, 17, 42, 101, 114, 127, 162. See Introduction, p. 15 f.

83

Byrhtwold, an old and trusty retainer (*eald genēat*), 309. He is conceivably identical with the Brihtwold, *cniht* of Æðelfiæd, Byrhtnoð's sister-in-law, who bequeathed him two hides of land at Donyland, Essex (BCS 1288, Whitelock xiv. 36/24). This identification would harmonize with the description of him as a *genēat*; see 309n.

Cēola, father of **Wulfstān,** 76. For his descendants, see under **Wulfstān.**

Dene, *pl.i-stem,* ' Danes '; **Denon,** *dat.* 129. The name *Dene* was sometimes given indiscriminately to Scandinavians in OE writings. The viking force at Maldon was predominantly Norwegian rather than Danish, though it may have included some adventurers from other Scandinavian realms.

Dunnere, a simple yeoman (*unorne ceorl*), who takes his stand with Byrhtnoð's noble retainers, 255.

Ēadric, one of Byrhtnoð's retainers, 11.

Ēadweard, one of Byrhtnoð's retainers, 117; **Ēadweard se langa,** 273, may or may not be the same person.

Ēadwold, retainer of Byrhtnoð, brother of **Ōswold,** 304.

Ealhelm, grandfather of Ælfwine, father-in-law of Ælfric, 218. The fuller form of his name is Ealhhelm. He was ealdorman of Mercia, and his name is found with the title *dux* on royal charters from c. 940 to c. 951 (BCS 757 and 891 and some fourteen others). See *Crawford Ch,* p. 88.

Ēastseaxe, *pl.i-stem,* East Saxons; **Ēastseaxena,** gen. 69. The *Eastseaxena ord* in 69 is the provincial *fyrd* of Essex.

Ecglāf, a Northumbrian of noble family, father of Æscferð, 267.

Gadd, kinsman of Offa, 287. The name *Gadd* is otherwise unknown in OE. It was perhaps originally weak, **Gadda,* corresponding to OHG *Gaddo, Gatto, Geddo, Ketto*; just as *Cēol* is found side by side with *Cēola* as a short form of names in *Cēol-*. *Gadd* might be a short form of such a name as *Gadferð,* or a nickname derived from the base of OE (*ge*)*gada, gædeling* ' companion '.

Godric (1), son of **Odda,** who fled from the battle on Byrhtnoð's horse, 187, 237, 325.

Godric (2), son of Æðelgār, one of Byrhtnoð's retainers who fought to the last, 321.

Godwīg, son of **Odda,** brother of **Godric** (1) and **Godwine,** 192.

Godwine, son of **Odda,** brother of **Godric** (1) and **Godwīg,** 192*. E has *Godrine,* which some editors emend to *Godrinc*; but that name is not authenticated.

Lēofsunu, retainer of Byrhtnoð, probably from Sturmer in Essex, 244.

Maccus, one of the three defenders of the *bricg,* 80. Maccus is a Celtic name, recorded from Cornwall in the second half of the tenth century in a list of manumissions (M. Förster, *Jespersen*

Miscellany, p. 91) and also in Ireland, Man and the Hebrides, where it is borne by persons of Scandinavian origin or descent. In Irish annals the same person is called both Magnus and Maccus, and it would seem that the Norse name Magnus, which is of quite distinct origin, was in Ireland equated with Maccus : see A. Bugge, *Vikingerne* II. 279–80. We may note also that the Maccus who fought at Maldon definitely antedates the first Norse Magnus. On other instances of *Maccus* in England, see A. H. Smith, *Revue Celtique* xliv. 44, and *Place-Names of Northamptonshire*, Eng. Place-Name Society, x. 237, sub *Maxey*. It is improbable that Byrhtnoð's Maccus came from the west of England, as Liebermann assumes, but we may guess that either he or one of his ancestors was a Norse viking from Ireland.

Myrce, *pl.i-stem*, the Mercians, Mercia ; **Myrcon,** *dat.* 217.

Norðhymbre, *pl.i-stem*, the Northumbrians, Northumbria ; **Norðhymbron,** *dat.* 266.

Odda, father of **Godric, Godwine** and **Godwīg**, 186, 238. The name Odda may be of Scandinavian origin (from ON *Oddi*), or it may be a short form of an English name beginning with *Ord-* (e.g. *Ordgār*). His sons all have native English names.

Offa, one of Byrhtnoð's chief officers, probably leader of the English after Byrhtnoð's death, 5, 198, 230, 286, 288.

Ōswold, one of Byrhtnoð's retainers, brother of **Ēadwold,** 304.

Pante, *w.f.* the river Blackwater in Essex, 68, 97. ' The old name Pant (pronounced Pont) is still applied to the river below Maldon '—E. Ekwall, *English River-Names*, p. 319. See also P. H. Reaney, *Place-Names of Essex*, p. 9.

Sībyrht, one of Byrhtnoð's retainers, brother of **Æðeric,** 282. Possibly identical with Sibriht, kinsman of Æðelflæd, Byrhtnoð's sister-in-law ; she bequeathed to him land at Wickford, Essex (BCS 1288, Whitelock xiv. 36/21).

Stūrmere, Sturmer in Essex, 249. The village of Sturmer takes its name from a pool (*mere*) in the Stour, and it is evident from the poet's use of the preposition *embe* ' around ' that he had in mind the *mere* itself, rather than any particular place corresponding to the modern village.

Þurstān, father of **Wīstān,** 298. From OEScand *Þurstæin*.

Wīgelm, 300*. Possibly the father of **Offa** ; see note.

Wīstān, one of Byrhtnoð's retainers, son of **Þurstān,** 297. This name is possibly a late form of the rather uncommon OE *Wīgstān*, but as the man seems to be of Scandinavian descent, his name is rather to be derived from OEScand *Wīstæin* (= OE *Wēohstān*).

Wulfmǣr (1), son of Byrhtnoð's sister, 113.

Wulfmǣr (2) **se geonga, Wulmǣr,** a young warrior, son of **Wulfstān,** 155, 183.

Wulfstān, son of **Cēola,** father of **Wulfmǣr se geonga,** and the leading defender of the *bricg*, 75, 79, 155. There is a will of Lēofwine, son of Wulfstān (*Crawford Ch*, p. 22), dated 998, and this Lēofwine was probably the son of Wulfstān who fell at Maldon. The will specifies lands at Kelvedon (8 miles north-east of Maldon), Markshall (4 miles north of Kelvedon), Purleigh (3 miles south of Maldon) and Barling (12 miles south-east of Maldon). The property at Purleigh extended nearly to the site of the battle, or possibly included it; see 75n. Napier and Stevenson suggest that the Wulfric, son of Lēofwine, who fell in battle in East Anglia in 1010, was a son of this Lēofwine. Lēofwine's will gives the name of Wulfstān's sister as Lēofwaru, and her son is called Ēadwold. Perhaps Lēofwaru's husband was the Ēadwold who fought at Maldon, or his brother Ōswold; these brothers were related to others among the retainers, according to line 306. An Eynsham charter (KCD 714) gives the information that Lēofwine had been given a manor at Shipford in Oxfordshire which Byrhtnoð had received from King Ēadgar, and Lēofwine had afterwards bequeathed it to Æðelmǣr, son of ealdorman Æðelweard, his (Lēofwine's) kinsman. As Æðelmǣr was also a kinsman of Byrhtnoð, Lēofwine and his father Wulfstān must have been related either by blood or marriage to Byrhtnoð.